WILL

10 Guiding principles for Women to Impact with Love and Leadership.

By:

Dr. R. Vijaya Saraswathy

WILL

10 Guiding principles for Women to Impact with Love and Leadership.

By:

Dr. R. Vijaya Saraswathy

MBA, M. Com, PGDMM, M.A. (English)

President, WE GIRLS NGO

CEO & Founder, Godwin Academy

Mother Teresa Award Winning Life Coach

Acclaimed Memory Guru of India

Inspirational Speaker & Soft Skills Trainer

Regional Partner - SpaceTrek 3 D Immersive Learning & Mobile Planetarium

Honorary Registrar, Indian Virtual University for Peace and Education

Current President, BNI Legacy Chapter, Bangalore

Vice-President, South India Operations, International Business Federation, Singapore

Vice-President, IWFCI, India

I dedicate this book with great gratitude and heartfelt thanks to

Almighty GOD

Take charge, when others give up!

Nothing is interesting, if you are not interested!

Be WILLING to walk alone. Many who started with you won't finish with you.

FOREWORD

Linking love with leadership is very rare, but when one thinks of women, one can subscribe to the phenomenon of Women in love and leadership.

Any initiative taken, be it leadership in entrepreneurship or life skills, people normally think of qualities such as passion, perseverance, patience, commitment, communication but somehow love, as an emotion, is not widely accepted as part of leadership, in fact sometimes love as an emotion in business is considered as a weakness. I have always wondered why this is so!

I take this opportunity to congratulate all women, be it mothers, home makers, professionals, entrepreneurs, or politicians for their courage and ability to continue in spite of the unrecognized and unacknowledged love and

WILL

leadership skills that every one of us, against all odds, has displayed during our lives.

Wishing success and happiness to all the women in their endeavors God Bless!

Dr. Vijaya Saraswathy, I hope your message reaches every woman.

Dr. Sumitra Iyengar
National Chairman (Emeritus) & President
International Women Federation of Commerce &
Industry, India

ACKNOWLEDGEMENT

I have been exuberant about writing this book, primarily because I am a woman and I love and respect women the most and, I admire every woman, who descends on this planet earth and experiences both love and leadership at her own pace, style, and rhythm. I urge to guide them with principles that will help them outshine!

A woman is charmingly endearing. She loves unconditionally and plays every role that she adorns with responsibility. She wears her heart on her sleeves. I admire her for her strength and determination.

Congratulations for your courage! Yes, the very reason you are reading this book shows that you are a courageous woman who loves to transform for the

WILL

better (double the courage if you are a gentleman and many thanks to you) committed and action oriented to excel both in Love and Leadership in this phase of your life.

This book as Ten Guiding Principles to build a dynamic you and encourages you to excel and add value to your love for loved ones and life plus value add your capabilities and leadership abilities and build self-love & self-esteem.

This book helps you to become a better entrepreneur. It supports self-introspection and inspires you to be better by making minor changes in your routine and major change in your mindset.

I recommend you to consider this book as the Holy Book that will help you transform into a dynamic person. Believe me, the efforts might go unnoticed but results won't. Who best can understand a woman than a woman herself?

These ten topics are time tested and the tools and techniques are used under various circumstances and found effective to build your inner strength from within. Take one topic at a time, read it, remember it, rehearse it, realize it, recall it during the test of times and most importantly use it and when it starts working make it a way of life.

This book is written to serve as a guide to help women of all ages who want to transform and improve their lives, willing to implement easily applicable mantras of love and leadership.

I want to thank my husband, children, my extended family and all the remarkable people present in my life - without your support, understanding, encouragement and care this journey would not have been possible.

Here we

Start, get, set go

COME WHAT MAY, GET UP, DRESS UP AND SHOW UP. AND NEVER, GIVE UP!

Celebrate self and be ready to welcome the new you!

CONTENTS

Foreword v

Acknowledgement vii

Introduction xii

Chapter 1 : Become Smart and Awaken the Creative Genius in You 1

Chapter 2 : Become Introspective and Discover the Peaceful You... 16

Chapter 3 : Become Sensitive to Time Expenditure............... 29

Chapter 4 : Become Systematic and Sort Stress 49

Chapter 5 : Become a Sincere and Dynamic Leader 60

WILL

Chapter 6 : Become a Storyteller and An Effective Communicator 94

Chapter 7 : Mind and Memory Management 118

Chapter 8 : Become Successful With Power Goals 128

Chapter 9 : Become a Sport and Deal with the Power of Health 139

INTRODUCTION

This book is exclusively for women; the purpose of writing this book is to inspire the women (YOU) to TRANSFORM your thoughts and take corrective action to put a ding in the universe.

This book also encourages women (you) to step up to the next rung of the ladder for experiencing the growth, abundance and success both in personal and professional life. The one and only life you have!

The Ten Guiding Principles are easy to understand, follow and apply if you take on and put to action everything suggested. Week after week you will see the difference, and appreciate the power of clarity and action.

WILL

Let me start with a universally compatible question

Give it a deep thought. Even if you have heard the question before, answer it today with your present mind-set and belief.

What is the purpose of your life?

Take time, think, think a little more and then, write down the answer. Make it into a statement - it should be concise. Make it a powerful statement: YOUR VISION STATEMENT.

The moment you realize your priorities, whatever the purpose, your purpose in life will become persistent. And the Vision Statement should be hovering before you. Pay attention to it, read it again. The sentence you are reading matters the most to you. Sometimes, our conscious mind needs provocation to achieve the set goals.

For anything remarkable to happen, you first have to put your mind to it and then, it will definitely happen.

Ask two more clarifying questions:

Is it easy to achieve your purpose of statement?

WILL

No? Fantastic, you are on the right track.

Probe further, is it worth? If the answer is YES, then wow! There's no looking back.

The objective of writing this book *WILL, Women in Love and Leadership* is to support you to strengthen the basics of leading powerfully, with unconditional love and committed leadership, to build a better and dynamic you. My vision statement is progressing to manifest. If you are willing to improve your leadership qualities and enhance the love quotient in your life, you are holding the right book in your hand: *WILL*.

Chapter 1

BECOME SMART AND AWAKEN THE CREATIVE GENIUS IN YOU

Do things boldly and consider your work noble.

Being a creative genius is a noble thought, noble action, noble feeling, noble habit and every noble work at first impossible.

It takes systems mindset and action to make it possible.

WILL

Your tongue print and palm print do not match with anyone else in this world. You are unique. Out of millions, you are one of a kind. When your existence is a spectacular marvel, live up to it, be a creative genius. *Love what you do and do what you love.*

Being a creative genius will do you good because you are measuring it in terms of love, trust me, it was wonderful for me and I am sure it is a great technique to adopt, act and appreciate and repeat the systems in every area of your life to obtain spectacular results.

First, introspect understand and know you what you are good at. How to make it GREAT?

There is actually a formula to calculate this:

Take your age, minus five years, whatever is the answer that is the number of years that you know yourself for.

Now analyze yourself how many of these categories of intelligence do you possess from this broad classification of Multiple Intelligences?

We all have broadly eight basic Multiple Intelligences in different proportions, namely:

WILL

1. Logical Intelligence
2. Language Intelligence
3. Articulate Intelligence
4. Musical Intelligence
5. Bodily Intelligence
6. Intrapersonal Intelligence
7. Interpersonal Intelligence
8. Musical Intelligence

Women with Logical Intelligence are exceptional at churning numbers and you love math, calculations and solving equations.

Women with Language Intelligence are amazing at oratory, debate, and public speaking and writing.

Women with Articulate Intelligence ability take the world by stride. They are able to express beautifully with choice of words and medium. They express their thoughts, action and feeling better than the others.

Women with Musical Intelligence are great musicians, singers and players of musical instruments.

Women with Bodily Intelligence are marvelous dancers, gymnasts, actors, and fitness instructors and sportspersons.

Women with Intrapersonal Intelligence are very spiritual and connect with their inner conscious frequently and know their attributes and basic characteristics well.

Intrapersonal Skills

One of the most important forms of intelligence that describes our personality and depicts our behavior is interpersonal skill.

Interpersonal skills are broadly divided into three types:

1. Passive
2. Aggressive
3. Assertive

Passive

During a passive behavior many women display cowardice attitude. She does not deal with the people with boldness.

Her behavior is indirect and communicates a message of inferiority. She will allow others to win and she will become subservient to the needs rights of others.

Most of the times she would feel herself to be a victim of the whims and fancies of others.

Allowing others to have their way, becoming subversive to the needs and rights of others and feeling victimized by others, conveying a message of inferiority and at times incompetence of self are some of the characteristics of this behavior.

Outcome: Lose - Win (one person loses, the other wins. Not a healthy style to practice).

Aggressive behavior

Now we shall analyze aggressive behavior, Opposite of passive behavior is aggressive behavior.

This type of behavior communicates superiority and disrespect; some women place their wants, needs and rights above those of others. Though aggressive women may win the deal but lose the sympathy and consideration of others. In the long run the loss is greater than the gain.

Outcome: Win – Lose or at times: Lose - Lose (Again, not a healthy style).

Assertive

Assertive is being active, direct, honest and also polite. This communicates an impression of self-respect, self-confidence and respect for others. This behavior leads to success without retaliation and encourages honest and open relationship.

Assertive behavior is when women view their wants, needs and rights as equal with those of others. Here women do not compete with men but themselves.

Envision a situation where you see yourself being assertive, feel confident, powerful, and effective, and hear your voice sound strong and steady. The more powerful your mental image and expectation, the greater the success you should experience.

Positive mental imagery is an exercise requiring conscious effort. This influences our subconscious mind and becomes one of our most challenging undertakings.

We Women are the top most emotional creatures. You can choose to be happy or depressed. It is in your own hands. Unfortunately, women do not realize that feeling are their own choices.

WILL

If you get angry, frightened of feeling sad over the words or actions of someone, you have no choice of your own. In this context the story of Sister Kenny is worth mentioning.

Sister Elizabeth Kenny, the famed Irish Australian nurse managed to stay constantly cheerful, no matter what the provocation was.

One day a friend asked her whether she was born calm and happy. She said, "No", and continued, "When I was little, my mother gave me a piece of advice which I have been following. Her advice was Anyone who angers you, conquers you. Anger is one letter short of DANGER."

Anger is our reaction to someone's action or inaction. But our reaction is a matter of our own choice. The best answer to provocation is inner silence.

People with assertive behavior are not disturbed emotionally by the words or action of others.

They keep their inner tranquility intact whatever be the situation. An assertive woman will not get angry at all and she will remain cool.

An aggressive woman gets angry quickly and openly expresses it. A passive person gets angry but does not expresses it, she burns inside. An assertive person will not get angry at all and is able to remain cool.

She will be very firm in her approach without losing her cool.

To communicate thoughts, feelings and opinions assertively, you need to choose words that are direct, honest, appropriate, and respectful.

Some words do not fit these criteria and therefore cannot be delivered assertively

Use "I statements" rather than "you statements". Example: "You always interrupt my talk!" is an aggressive statement. It can be paraphrased in the following manner, "I would like to talk to you without interruption" is an assertive statement.

Assertive behavior does not use the strategy of hinting, indirect mentioning of or presuming things. You can increase your success rate and improve relationships by using direct, honest and assertive words.

Staying aware of all aspects of body language continuously is not possible. Having some awareness is very important if you want to develop the virtue of assertive behavior.

WILL

Assertive behavior demands greater care in using body language. More than the words, HOW YOU SAY THEM is highly essential for assertive behavior. Your delivery of the message makes all the difference. This is known as body language. Everything becomes important when a message is being delivered: voice, tone, volume, inflection, pace, eye contact or lack of it, facial expression, gestures, movements or lack thereof, posture, muscle tension, clothing, hairstyle, eyeglasses, etc.

You don't have to constantly monitor all aspects of body language to be assertive. You need to learn some body language signals to accompany your words that would help others to perceive your assertive behavior. Be positive and assertive.

Experience the satisfaction and pleasure of being assertive and do it repeatedly. Make it a habit.

Win by influencing, listening, and understanding. Others co-operate willingly. This encourages honest and open relationships.

Outcome: Win - Win

WILL

You can actually check for yourself how you fare on these classifications of intelligence which are logical, language oriented, articulate, bodily, musical, interpersonal, intrapersonal and naturalistic.

I have also given you the best tool to use, the best interpersonal tool and that is assertiveness.

Fortunately, I think there is one more wonderful intelligence tool, which is the best tool for all us women if we want to excel. If we master this intelligence we will win every battle we fight with confidence.

Read this part of the book when you choose to be happy, receptive and introspective. Don't read it if you are stressed, angry or sad.

The intelligence which I love, learn and leverage is Emotional Intelligence:

- Capacity for recognizing our own feelings and those of others for motivating ourselves and others in our relationships.
- Emotional intelligence is distinct from, but complementary to academic intelligence (IQ).
- Feelings to be identified to guide us through thoughts and action.

WILL

1. Self-Awareness: Knowing what we are thinking and feeling at the moment. Using it to guide our decision-making capabilities.
   Have a realistic assessment of our own abilities and a well-grained sense of self-confidence.
2. Self-Regulation: Handling our emotions so that they facilitate rather than interfere with the task at hand (or performance) pursuing goals, recovering well from emotional distress.
3. Empathy: Sensing what people are feeling and ability to take their perspective.
   Cultivating rapport with a broad diversity of people.
4. Motivation: Using our deepest preference to move and guide us towards our goals. Help us take initiative and strive to improve. Persevere in the face of setbacks and frustrations.
5. Social Skills: Handling emotions in relationship well. Reading social situations and networks accurately. Interacting smoothly.

Use these skills to persuade and lead, negotiate, settle disputes and to establish team spirit.

Remember, today is the first day for the rest of your life, Celebrate Life!

WILL

Life will always rise and fall,
No matter what you never forget to smile at all!

Dr. R. Vijaya Saraswathy

Action Plan

How do we Develop Creative Ideas? An Action Plan

1. Develop an attitude to be creative.
2. Search for new ideas based on your past knowledge and experience.
3. Try various approaches.
4. If you are not able to get anywhere, try some crazy, foolish, impractical and even useless ideas.
5. Break the rules occasionally.
6. Explore for ideas outside your field of work.
7. Have the faith that truth is all around, you have to explore according to your needs and requirements.
8. The best way to get good ideas is to get a lot of ideas through brainstorming. You may not be able to use all of them but of the number you

generate, you may find a few that are worthwhile.

9. For development of creative ideas follow an imaginative phase and also a practical phase. The motto of imaginative phase is to generate and play with ideas and that of practical phase is to evaluate the ideas generated and execute them.

10. Be an artist and also a judge. The open-minded attitude of the artist typifies the kind of thinking you use in the imaginative phase when you are generating ideas. The evaluative outlook of the judge represents the kind of thinking you use in the practical phase when you are preparing ideas for execution.

11. Frame a few "what if" questions. Example: What if animals became more intelligent than people? What if a world famous magician made *WILL* disappear from your hand all of a sudden? The "as if" questions will stimulate the thinking process and thereby facilitate for the generation of some useful creative ideas. It is also a powerful way to get your imagination going.

12. Challenge the rules, if necessary. This does not mean that you should do anything illegal, immoral and unethical. Don't fall in love with a

certain approach. Then you will not be able to see the merits of alternative approaches.

13. Necessity is the mother of invention but playful attitude is certainly its father. When you are in a playful mood, your defenses are down but mental blocks are loosened, concern for rules is absent, practicality is given the backseat, no guilty conscience for being wrong, when you win you win and when you lose you learn.

14. Group thinking may not be very conducive for generating creative ideas. In a group, people would tend to get approval of others.

15. If you enjoy what you do you will come up with more ideas.

16. Get in a humorous frame of mind, which not only loosens you up, but also enhances your creativity.

17. Using metaphorical language with fun and humor would add colour and flavor to creativity.

18. Example (deliberately chosen from cooking – WE WOMEN ROCK): Life is like a *Vada*. It is delicious when it is fresh and warm. It will be hard if not cooked properly. The hole in the middle is a mystery. Without that hole it won't be a *Vada*. HAVE FAITH IN YOUR ABILITY TO BE CREATIVE

WILL

AND YOU WILL GENERATE PERENNIAL FLOW OF CREATIVE IDEAS.

19. Write your own creative idea in the **space below:**

Chapter 2

BECOME INTROSPECTIVE AND DISCOVER THE PEACEFUL YOU

A woman told Buddha, "I want happiness."
Buddha said, "Knock out I from your sentence."

In I want happiness, I is the EGO.

She was left with "want happiness".

Buddha said, "Knock out want for it is desire."

She now had ONLY HAPPINESS.

What is the Alpha Waves of Mental State?

Mind emits some kind of electrical waves on the basis of the metabolic functioning of the body. The scientists who study the human mechanism were able to detect and measure the existence of these waves. A gadget called electroencephalograph (EEG) is used to measure the pattern of emitting these waves. They are categorized into four types, viz.

1. BETA WAVES
2. ALPHA WAVES
3. THETA WAVES, and
4. DELTA WAVES

These waves are measured in terms of certain number of cycles per second. When the mental cyclic waves go beyond 14 cycles per second, they are called Beta waves. They are being emitted when a person is in the wakeful state with full of activity of one kind or the other. Alpha Waves are noticed when they are between 7 and 14 cycles per second. The mental state at this level is said to be calm and quiet, cool and collected, serene and tranquil. This is the state of the mind which is said be more productive and creative. Theta Waves are measured between 4 and 7 cycles per second. It is a state of drowsiness of the mind. The consciousness of the person is blurred. This is a state before deep sleep. When a person has deep sleep he emits Delta waves, which are below 4 cycles per second. At this state the person is totally unaware of his external stimuli.

Importance of Alpha Waves

A totally relaxed phase of the mind is called Alpha Waves of mental state. The productivity and creativity of a person will be at its peak when the mind reaches Alpha state. This is the best time to take important decisions. One is in a happy frame of mind. Negative feelings and attitudes are completely eschewed from the consciousness. It is the most desirable state of mind. Alpha Waves cannot be present when a person is in a depressed and is in a stressful situation.

How to Reach the Alpha Waves State of Mind?

Women must reach this state of mind every day before going to sleep. When a woman does not get sleep due to stress, tension, anxiety and worries, she will not reach the Alpha Waves of mental state. Therefore, she cannot get peaceful sleep. Only in the absence of stress and worries, a person can reach Alpha State and then slips into slumber. All meditation techniques bring Alpha

WILL

Waves. The practitioner of meditation will not find any difficulty to reach Alpha Waves of mental state.

The most difficult problem for any person is to maintain Alpha State of the mind most of the time. These are possible by living in the present and also by practicing AWARE and BEWARE technique.

To become aware, ask the below question (please do not read the answer, till you come up with your own first):

WHY DO WE SLEEP?

Once you are convinced of your answer, read the answer below;

Yes! I got your answer beautiful lady, the body needs rest, relaxation, to pep up for the next day. With all these right answers if we probe further. The reality is that, most importantly Almighty God wants you to REHEARSE FOR YOUR DEATH. He is making us AWARE Everyday that we are here for a purpose and we need to go back. We are not permanent here; the truth is no one was!

The moment you are born you are walking towards the grave. You are not alone. Anyone who is alive as of now in this planet earth is definitely walking towards the grave. It doesn't matter how old or young, it doesn't matter sick or healthy, It doesn't matter poor or rich, it doesn't matter bad or good person. The moment you become AWARE that you are practicing every day for your death, the very perspective of life changes. You are in Alpha state of mind most of the times; you become aware whatever happens in your life you have only 10% influence over it, the rest 90% is how you give your reaction to it. If we get into this right attitude, not positive or negative we are in the right track of being AWARE.

Constant vigilance of the mental processes is needed to maintain this state of being AWARE.

Every culture has used some technique for restricting awareness to a single, unchanging source of stimulation for a more or less lengthy period of time. This restriction of attention is used for a variety of purposes: to attain a state of ecstasy, gain spiritual insight, escape pain and suffering, obtain new wisdom, enhance creativity, gain access to special mental and physical powers, improve health or alleviate sickness, become one with the universal force, increase sensory acuity, cleanse the door of perception, become a better human being. Specific techniques are many. Buddhists concentrate on their breathing.

Being in Alpha state of mind is a process of shifting the consciousness from self to something else. It is to be treated as a way of life. It is not a question of doing but a state of being. In order to reach the state of being, meditating is necessary. Such doing is called the Alpha state of mind techniques. The best and easily adoptable method is meditation.

Meditation is the most profound method of being silent: It helps you enhance your inner glow inside out. While the inner glow are influenced by your:

1. Intuition
2. Knowledge
3. Thinking
4. Behavior
5. Aptitude
6. Presence of mind
7. Attitude

Women should adopt silencing their inner self ranging from 5 minutes to 55 minutes a day as per their convenience, from below you can choose from 16 varieties of meditation. You can mix and match, pick and choose or be loyal to one method:

1. Intention Meditation – just sit with an intention to meditate. It is the simplest form and takes a minimum of 5 minutes.
2. Sound Meditation – being aware of the sound, 7 minutes.
3. Thoughtful Meditation – being aware of the thoughts that are surfacing the consciousness, 9 minutes.
4. Attribute Meditation – being aware of an object, symbol, 12 minutes.
5. Soham Meditation – repetition of the word So-Ham, synchronizing with inhalation and exhalation, 15 minutes.
6. Bhagya Kumbhaka Meditation – being aware of the outer retention, 18 minutes.
7. Transcendental Meditation – It is a mantra yoga meditation – repeating a mantra silently, 21 minutes.
8. Jnana Yoga Meditation – asking a series of question pertaining to life, death, creation, etc., 30 minutes.
9. Subconscious Meditation – saturate the mind with sublime thoughts – repetition of certain

quotations, which are effective to inspire for better living, 40 minutes.

10. Water Boat Meditation – traveling in a water boat visualization – 45 Minutes
11. Why Do You Sleep Meditation – observing your own body as dead and being burnt in a pyre, 45 minutes.
12. Cycle Meditation – being aware of the breathing and count its cycles, 50 minutes.
13. Creative Dynamic Mind Mediation – combination of a variety of meditation techniques, 55 minutes
14. Numerical Meditation – Registering and reproducing 100 digit numbers, as per convenience.
15. Self Development Meditation – Repeating positive attributes – "I am Able ...", as per convenience.
16. Memory Filing Technique Meditation – recollecting all the memory files created by you, as per convenience.

Create your own combination meditation and write your feelings after meditating.

Action Plan

Mindfulness. The action plan after meditation is mindfulness.

Mindfulness is optimistic observation of self, environment and people around you. The positive vibration you send and receive manifests your dreams into reality.

Mindfulness is like constructing a beautiful house and meditation is like maintaining the built house.

Mindfulness is:

1. Making an inward journey.
2. A process of stilling the mind.
3. Introspection of self is mindfulness.
4. Emptying the mind (It's full and you are clearing the clutter).
5. It is taking away our consciousness from external entanglement.
6. An altered state of consciousness (Alpha State).
7. Making peace with the inner self.
8. The barrier between the conscious and subconscious mind is removed.

9. It establishes a link between the higher regions of the mind and the waking consciousness.
10. It is shifting the consciousness from self to something productive.
11. The mindfulness provides you revival through So-Ham and degrees of breath works and Meditation helps you retain the momentum.
12. Mindfulness being, alert, alive and happy always.

Benefits

Mindfulness benefits us in several ways:

1. Brings profound relaxation.
2. Slows down metabolic rate, that is, the rate at which the body burns oxygen and food necessary for building up the body.
3. Heart rate slows down.
4. Blood flow increases due to reduction in the constriction of blood vessels.
5. Due to increased blood flow, lactic acid produced during intense activity quickly and effectively reduced.
6. Lactic acid production is less when one is calm and serene

7. Persons experiencing anxiety, stress and tension have a high level of lactic acid, which is one of the symptoms of high blood pressure.
8. Reduction in lactic acid level leads to deep relaxation, which consequently reduces high blood pressure.
9. Brings about improvement in psychosomatic diseases.
10. Improves memory, intelligence and emotional stability.
11. Brings mental discipline and thereby improving one's temperament with better social and vocational adjustment.
12. Being mindful makes you physiologically powerful.
13. Mindfulness brings far better and profound perceptions.
14. The natural corollary of the constant practice of mindfulness is the inner peace and harmony.
15. The stormy turmoil of the ebb and flow of the emotional torments of everyday living are subsided and neutralized with the onset of deep meditation.
16. During mindfulness changes take place for better with regard to brain rhythm (production of Alpha Waves), blood pressure pulse rate, etc.

17. Profound impact in curing incurable diseases like cancer. Dr. Carl Simonton of USA has cured hundreds of terminal cancer patients through his CRVR Meditation Technique.

Some Practical Tips on Mindfulness

1. Mindfulness should be taken more as a way of life than a mere ceremony to be performed piously at an appointed time.
2. Efforts should be made to fully occupy the mind always with pure and positive thoughts.
3. The mind should be allowed to attend only one thing at a time.
4. Any wakeful state could be utilized for mindfulness.
5. Even while traveling in a car, train, bus or plane mindfulness can be practiced.
6. The essence of mindfulness can be summed up in two words – AWARE and BEWARE. During the awake state the practitioner should be aware of his thoughts, feelings and actions.
7. The moment the thought, word, emotion, or action slips down to negative or impure aspects, one should be aware and banish it immediately.

8. Instead of brooding over personal problems, it is better to concentrate on some constructive activities intended to bring some beneficial results to oneself and to the humanity at large.
9. The mind should always be saturated with the theme "Love for all and hatred towards none". No event, however adverse, should disturb the mind. It should always be peaceful, tranquil and serene.
10. Mindfulness is creating a divine aura of body, mind and soul and meditation is the maintenance mechanism of the built aura. Maintain its beauty by arresting the block of *chakras*.
11. Mindfulness helps you to think and act effectively.
12. Mindfulness helps you discard anger, anxiety and frustrations.

Chapter 3

BECOME SENSITIVE TO TIME EXPENDITURE

Live in the Present

Our main business in life is not to see what lies dimly at a distance but to do what lies clearly at hand.

- Dale Carnegie

Time is the dimension in which changes take place. Whatever is happening in this world is due to the existence of time. Nothing can happen overnight. Time has the role to play in all the changes that take place in this world.

WILL

Time is measurable. It is measured in terms of seconds, minutes, hours, days, weeks, years, centuries, etc. Because of its measurable nature time can be quantitatively expressed. The watch that we wear is one of the instruments to measure time.

Time spent is time saved. Only when you spend the time fruitfully you can save the time. In other words, time, which is spent usefully, will help you to achieve your goals in life.

Time moves faster when you are happy and slower when you are depressed or unhappy. You do not realize the passage of time when you are in the company of loved ones, the reason being you are happy during that time. Psychologically you feel that the time is spent very fast. On the other hand, when you spend your time with a person you inherently hate, you seem to have spent the time longer than what it actually is, because you are not happy in that person's company.

Woman who value time, celebrate life. Time is the most precious commodity available to us is time. Time cannot be deposited for future nor withdrawn for want of it. Time the only commodity every living being gets in uniform universally irrespective of their age, caste, gender, class, and country. Being an inspirational trainer,

WILL

I deal with this topic with passionately. I regard time to be the most valuable element. Time seems to go more slowly in dark than in light. During daytime or in full bright light, people are busy with one activity or the other. While in darkness the activity of the individual is reduced. In the absence of any activity time moves very slowly in darkness.

Time is valued more as we age. The perception of youngsters in general is that they are going to live for a long time. Whereas old people will normally visualize that their years to live is shorter. Therefore, aged people consider time to be more precious than the youngsters. Time is a relative concept. It cannot be considered as an entity. Time is the most precious of our possessions. We operate our life in time. The way in which we spend the time determines the quality of our life. People normally consider time as a precious possession. Since it is given to everyone equally its preciousness is not valued.

When one says that time flies or time drags time but merely it is our experience of time at a particular moment. Time is finite. Nobody has any more of it than you, i.e. 24 hours a day, 168 hours per week, and 8,760 hours per year. What really counts is how you make use of it. Time will not wait for us. We may choose to let it pass or use each moment to the fullest extent possible.

There is no free sample of time. Time is spent in everything we do. Time is money in the sense that, let us put it in a simple way for a tribal woman who is earning a monthly income of Rs. 6,000 each hour costs about Rs. 8.33 and the same calculation may be applied to each of us.

Time is the period during which action or process continues. If we are not active, it is presumed that time is wasted. It becomes quite obvious that time is intended to do something useful either to the society or to your own personal needs. Time is the most predictable resource at the disposal of anyone. Unfortunately it is the most neglected, misused and mismanaged resource.

Time is the fourth dimension. Material objects exist in three dimensions of breadth, width and depth. Things exist because of time. The concept of time as the fourth dimension is slightly difficult to understand. This can be explained through an illustration. Imagine I want to cross the road. A minute back a lorry passed that road. Had I crossed the road at that time, the lorry would have crushed me. I crossed the road only after the passing of the lorry. I continue to live because of the time factor.

WILL

Therefore, in all our existence, time is considered as the fourth dimension.

I urge you set priorities, prepare a to-do-list, concentrate on activities bringing rich dividends.

The crucial decision is to classify time into:

- Personal focus
- Official focus

Schedule time for each activity and maintain a log, which is:

1. Clear
2. Well-defined
3. Realistic
4. Time-bound
5. Based on one's strengths
6. Clear-cut, and
7. Is reviewed on a daily basis.

Maintain an activity log, which defines your time expenditure of time.

Many of my friends ask me Vijaya, "How do you manage so many things? You are all over the place!" Your education is ever continuing, you are a part of so many

WILL

forums and associations, you run Godwin Academy, run so many training programs for colleges and corporate houses, how do you manage?

I always tell them I only manage my time; and my time manages everything for me.

Schedule your time on hourly basis for a week and see the difference.

For instance:

5.30 to 6.30 – Wake up, attend nature's call and complete meditation.

6.30 to 7.30 – Have coffee, read as per schedule, plan your wear, etc.

You schedule the entire day for a week and review your activity every four hours you know where your time pilferage is. The moment you realize where the time is spent unnecessarily you can take timesaving actions. Automatically, after week awareness get imbibed in your system.

Always have a things-to-do list and it based on that allot your time for the work. Prioritize:

WILL

1. Urgent work,
2. Important work,
3. Important work but not urgent now,
4. Urgent now but not important,
5. Urgent and important.

Think on these terms; prioritize as per your mindset, convenience and nature of work.

The moment you write down the categories you will find unique ways to allot time and complete the task.

Develop time consciousness. A good understanding of time is required for this.

Formulate goals and objectives. Internal and external goals – update your goals on Activity Log on daily, weekly and monthly basis and review it to enhance your performance.

The final outcome should be to achieve the following:

At *personal focus* level:

1. Enhance your personal qualities
2. Develop assertive behavior
3. Avoid procrastination by repeating the sentence - begin and the work will be completed.

WILL

4. Be punctual
5. Discard perfectionism
6. Develop team spirit
7. Motivate yourself – appreciate freedom and function independently

Organize your personal life, maintain good health, spend time with family members, relax, read books and journals, attend important work during peak energy hours.

At *official focus* level:

1. Modify time consuming procedures,
2. Train your staff,
3. Refine professional skills, learn latest online trends, write effective emails, and prepare brilliant reports.
4. Communicate effectively, and learn speed-reading.
5. Acquire memory skills and memorize top client details.
6. Deal with interruptions and unexpected visitors.
7. Take one project at a time.
8. Organize professional life, attend meetings with proper agendas, maintain proper filing system, delegate judiciously and streamline paperwork.

WILL

Do you love your life?

Dear Dynamic Lady,

How do you begin each day? At what hour do you rise? How do you commence your duties? In what frame of mind do you enter upon the sacred life of a new day? What answer can you give your heart to these important questions? You will find that much happiness follows upon the right or wrong beginning of the day, and that, when every day is wisely begun, happy and harmonious sequences will mark its course, and life in its totality will not fall short of the ideal blessedness.

The way you elect to spend your time determines the quality of your life.

If you want to improve your quality of life, then do not squander time, for that is the stuff life is made of. Even gold worth tons of money is not as valuable as a single moment in one's life. Therefore, he who wastes his time is committing a serious crime.

If you choose to live a full life, you must appreciate the importance of time and of self-discipline. Appropriate utilization of time enables you to enjoy both your work and your leisure. Self-discipline means will power to do

WILL

those things you know should be done before doing the things you want to do because they are more enjoyable. By tackling rather than procrastinating, you will often find time enough to do both. Since it is your time you are spending, you should master your time, do not let it master you. And you can't master your time until you're first willing to master yourself. That is why leadership is a part and parcel of this book

Are you earnest? Seize this very minute; what you can do or dream, you can achieve what you dream; boldness has genius, power and magic in it. Practice and follow, and perseverance becomes a habit; begin and the work will be completed.

Time management is attractive to busy people. People are interested in achieving something in life. Their busy schedule is normally synchronized with productive activity. Time management provides the methods and techniques to utilize the time usefully. Therefore, people who are achievement-oriented will be interested in time management.

Time supply is gloriously regular but cruelly restricted. When you wake up in the morning you have twenty-four hours ahead of you to spend. The supply of 24 hours to you is very regular. Whether you like it or not, you will get 24 hours every day. This amount of time is also restricted. You will not get even one second more than the normal supply of time.

Time cannot be made or manufactured. Time just exists. We live in time. There is no question of either production or manufacture of time. Time is in eternity. There is no beginning or end for time. Time looms large when attention is bestowed on it. When a person is in total concentration time passes very fast. When a person is bored with a lecture, he looks at his watch at frequent intervals. In such a situation, time seems to be stretched beyond its normal course.

Time is the raw material of all our achievements. If you are seriously interested in doing something great and outstanding in life, you should consider each and every second of your wakeful state as precious and invaluable. This type of consciousness will motivate you to utilize your time most productively and creatively.

TIME MANAGEMENT IS NOTHING BUT ORGANIZED WAY OF DOING THINGS - UTILIZING EACH AND EVERY SECOND OF OUR EXISTENCE.

Action Plan for Managing the Seven Time Zones:

Life is divided into seven time zones. If one needs complete fulfillment in life she has to balance all the seven zones without any imbalance. Of late we are used to do certain things in excess and never touch some things, which we ought to do. All said and done, we must give the body and mind what it desires. We must not over do things and follow the law of temperance.

The Seven Time Zones Categorized are:

- Family Time Zone
- Work Time Zone
- Spiritual Time Zone
- Psychological Time Zone
- Pleasure Time Zone
- Leisure Time Zone
- Twilight Time Zone.

Speaking about the seven time zones, we must balance all the seven in this manner:

Family Time Zone

Spend time with family and shower love on them, care

for them, share our thoughts. Save time by maintaining good, friendly relations, this way neither will we trouble people nor get troubled by them

Work Time Zone

We must do justice to our work without being told to do so. We must not spend too much time in it or for that matter laze away if no one is around.

Spiritual Time Zone

We must be one with God and follow his precepts and making sure that we remember God always and not only when we are in a difficulty. We must be clean not only physically but also mentally. We must inculcate a habit to devote time to this zone to feel peaceful and healthy.

Psychological Time Zone

This is a very important zone, which constitutes our complete mental balance pertaining to our thoughts, behavior and what we actually become in life. We have to tap the potential that is hidden within us. This is one zone that can take you to the top of the ladder. Invest a decent amount of time here, believe me, you will never regret.

Pleasure Time Zone

In this zone some of us over use time. The reason could be excess wealth or a penchant for wasting or whiling away time. We may earn money and waste it all and even borrow and go out of our means to satisfy our senses. This is one zone that has made millionaires paupers overnight.

Leisure Time Zone

Man after working needs rest. Even God after creating the world had some rest and he advised us to do the same.. We need not work six days and then rest but we can do it every day. It could be sleeping, watching a television or even taking a walk or going to a place which can be accessed by no body but you.

Twilight Time Zone

This is the last zone of our life. It is in this zone that we have to mellow down and go slow in whatever we do. Be it eating, sleeping or even taking a break. One must not depend on the children but be self-sufficient and leave a fortune for the kith and kin. We must yearn to leave our bodies in the most peaceful manner.

We must balance them without tilting any one of them. Prioritize them as and when they plunge. Do not engage in excesses.

Make your own PIE CIRCLE and allot your TIME ZONES. While computing your time zone take age, gender, economic independence and basic responsibilities into consideration.

Test Your TMQ (Time Management Quotient)

The following is a creative game that you can play to find out your Time Management Quotient. You have been managing your time in one way or the other. The following are some of the statements for which you have to give your response on a 10-point scale. All the statements are in question form. If the answer is "YES" you have to mark between 6 and 10. If your answer is "NO", you can mark between 0 and 4. For the question you are not able to decide mark 5. Your answer cannot be absolute. It must be relative. Therefore, you can make your choices between 0 to10. Play this game as sincerely and honestly as possible

0   1   2   3   4   5   6
**   7   8   9   10**

WILL

Mark your score here:

1. Do you consider that Time is the SCARCEST RESOURCE in your life?
2. Do you think that GOLD worth tons of money is not as valuable as a single minute?
3. Do you have the tendency to SEIZE every minute of your life for productive and creative purposes?
4. Do you have the GOALS written down that are obtainable and objectively quantifiable?
5. Do you know clearly your INTERNAL and EXTERNAL goals? Internal goals refer to improving certain skills, abilities, knowledge, character, etc. and external goals are your achievements in terms of targets and projects to be measured in quantitative terms?
6. Do you TRANSLATE your goals and projects into monthly, weekly and daily activities?
7. Do you maintain Time Management log? (an assessment of how you spend your time)
8. Do you update your goals and strategies?
9. Are you aware of the LIMITATIONS of your time frame?
10. Do you allow TIME CUSHION to provide for eventualities?

WILL

11. Do you keep CONSTANT COMPANION (C.C. a small note book) to check up the to-do-list every morning?
12. Do you undertake the GROUP RELATED activities at a stretch?
13. Do you organize your professional and personal life with some SYSTEM of your own. (Example: Keep everything in its own place)
14. Do you recognize INTUITIVELY what you should not do which would waste your time unnecessarily?
15. Do you tactfully avoid the DEMANDS OF OTHERS on your time?
16. Do you display ASSERTIVENESS when occasion demands?
17. Do you avoid PROCRASTINATION (postpone your work)?
18. Are you PUNCTUAL for all your appointments in professional and personal life?
19. Do you attempt PERFECTIONISM?
20. Do you apply PARETO'S RULE? (20% of what you do would bring 80% of the results. Therefore, concentrate only on 20%).
21. Do you MOTIVATE your staff to do better?
22. Do you make an attempt that your staff should not DEPEND too much on you?

23. Do you avoid involving yourself in the FRICTION amongst your staff?
24. Do you take any serious steps to avoid ABSENTEEISM among your staff?
25. Have you done anything to modify time consuming PROCEDURES into speedier ones?
26. Do you provide constant TRAINING to your staff for developing their knowledge and skills?
27. Do you know the operation of an android phone and are you proficient using online apps?
28. Do you RELAX during your free time without any feelings of guilt?
29. Do you purchase and read BOOKS and JOURNALS related to your profession?
30. Do you have the knowledge of Biorhythm Cycles and attend to your most important work during PEAK ENERGY HOURS?
31. Do you draft simple and effective emails?
32. Do you prepare your brilliant REPORTS (documentation of your activities) effectively and on time?
33. Do you COMMUNICATE, both oral and written, in a simple, understandable and effective manner?
34. Do you know the principles and practice of SPEED READING?

WILL

35. Do you have any techniques to enhance your MEMORY skills?
36. Do you know the code (Activity Log) and formula (Schedule Time) of MONTHLY CALENDAR PLANNER as a time saving device and apply it in your day-to-day life?
37. Do you tactfully deal with unexpected VISITORS who interrupt your work?
38. Do you effectively handle all your mobile calls/communication apps?
39. Do you practice the principles of STRESS Management (Meditation & Mindfulness)?
40. Do you prepare TIME BUDGET for every unit of work?
41. Do you prepare a series of ACTION PLANS and review it?
42. Are you making use of your mobile/diaries to monitor your time budget?
43. Do you REVIEW your work at frequent intervals in terms of your time budget?
44. Do you devote all your attention to ONE PROJECT at a time?
45. Do you attend MEETINGS with proper agenda and preparation?
46. Do you adopt a project FILING system?

WILL

47. Do you DELEGATE your work judiciously and appropriately?
48. Do you streamline your PAPER WORK?
49. Do you take proper care to maintain good HEALTH?
50. Do you spend sufficient time with your FAMILY members?

Total Score Obtained

Assess your Time Management Quotient:

You are expected to be very honest and sincere in your assessment of score values. Total the scores that you have obtained.

The maximum that a person can get is 500 and the minimum could be 0. Your score should range between these two. If you have scored more than 250, you are managing your time very effectively and less than 250 is an indication that you have to take necessary steps to improve your ability to manage your time.

Chapter 4

BECOME SYSTEMATIC AND SORT STRESS

Sorting stress is all about becoming aware what is stressing you and healing yourself. Process your unprocessed thoughts. Let go your past, enjoy your present and stop worrying about your future.

If you are sad, you are thinking about your past.

If you are anxious, you are thinking about your future.

Be in the present that is why it is called gift.

Enjoy the now!

WILL

That is why I love and repeat this beautiful rhyme multiple times in a day!

Sing along,

The time to be happy is now

The place to be happy is here

And the way to be happy is to make someone happy and bring a little heaven right here.

The time to be happy is NOW!

Now let's analyze what causes stress, why have we taken life so seriously. We have been very critical about self. If we face the difficult situations with the right attitude, stress can be sorted and conquered.

According to a research in 1967 the reasons for stress where analyzed and presented by T. H. Holmes & Rahe, Although it is a study done in the '60s, it still stands relevant, just take a look at the statistics.

STRESS PRODUCING SITUATIONS IN LIFE

As per the research conducted by Holmes & Rahe in 1967

WILL

	THE REASON FOR STRESS	% of stress
1	Death of spouse	100
2	Divorce	73
3	Marital separation from mate	65
4	Detention in jail or other institution	63
5	Death of a close family member	63
6	Major personal injury or illness	53
7	Marriage	50
8	Being fired from work	47
9	Marital reconciliation with mate	45
10	Retirement	45
11	Major change in the health or behavior of a family member	44
12	Pregnancy	40
13	Sexual difficulties	39
14	Gaining a new family member (birth or adoption)	39
15	Major business RE-adjustments (merger, reorganization, bankruptcy)	39
16	Major change in financial state	38
17	Death of a close friend	37
18	Changing to a different line of work	36

19	Arguments with spouses	35
20	Loans more than 20 times your monthly income	31
21	Repayment of loan	30
22	Major change in responsibilities in work (promotion, demotion, etc.)	29
23	Son or daughter leaving home	29
24	In-laws troubles	29
25	Outstanding personal achievements	28
26	Wife beginning or ceasing work outside the home	26
27	Beginning or ceasing formal schooling	26
28	Major change in leaving conditions (new home, etc.)	25
29	Revision of habits	24
30	Troubles with the boss	23
31	Major change in working hours or conditions	20
32	Change in residence	20
33	Changing to a new school	20
34	Major change in usual type of recreation	19
35	Major change in church activities	19

36	Major change in social activities	18
37	Taking a loan less in than 5 months salary	17
38	Major change in sleeping habits	16
39	Major change in number of family get-together	15
40	Major change in eating habits	15
41	Occasion	13
42	Christmas, festivals	12
43	Minor violation of law (traffic rules)	11

You need to realize your pain to get rid of your pain, knowing the cause of the pain becomes so much more important to address it, heal it and get better; likewise you should be aware of your stress to sort your stress and release it. So let go and start life with a new perspective.

Remember, my perception about you is the reflection of your own thoughts. You will find great relief, if you are disturbed if you read this story.

Buddha was once traveling with a few of his followers.

WILL

While they were passing a lake, Buddha told one of his disciples, "I am thirsty. Do get me some water from the lake."

A disciple walked up to the lake. At that moment, a bullock cart started crossing through the lake. As a result, the water became very muddy and turbid.

The disciple thought, "How can I give this muddy water to Buddha to drink?" So he came back and told Buddha, "The water in there is very muddy. I don't think it is fit to drink."

After about half an hour, again Buddha asked the same disciple to go back to the lake. The disciple went back, and found that the water was still muddy. He returned and informed Buddha about the same.

After sometime, Buddha again asked the same disciple to go back.

This time, the disciple found the mud had settled down, and the water was clean and clear. So he collected some water in a pot and brought it to Buddha. Buddha looked at the water, and then he looked up at the disciple and said, "See what you did to make the water clean. You let it be, and the mud settled down on its own, and you have clear water."

Your mind is like that too! When it is disturbed, just let it be. Give it a little time. It will settle down on its own. You don't have to put in any effort to calm it down. It will happen. It is effortless.

Having 'Peace of Mind' is not a strenuous job.

Affirmations for Sorting Stress

I wonder when people say stress management. I strongly believe stress is not something to be managed, but definitely be sorted.

We don't retain and manage garbage. If we do retain garbage for a couple of days the entire house will stink of it. Similarly, we don't manage stress, like garbage we should sort and discard it.

I follow these affirmations, which help me thrash my stress. It is simple, use it and you would definitely love it!

Repeat the following affirmations to sort stress on a daily basis:

WILL

1. **I firmly believe that I have the potential for** *Creative Genius.*
2. **I shall reach and maintain** *Alpha Waves of Mental State* **and thereby generate Creative Ideas most of the time.**
3. *My time* **is the precious currency of my life, which I utilize most productively and creatively.**
4. **I shall** *cherish an ideal* **and devote myself for its realization.**
5. **I shall be so** *engrossed in a project* **that I will simply not allow myself to become ill or indisposed.**
6. **I shall seal the dead past, not to worry about the unborn future, but live and enjoy the** *realistic present.*
7. **I fully believe that the only competition worthy of me is with myself. No one is superior to** me; **no one is inferior to me.** *I am what I am.*
8. **I strongly endorse the view that** *success* **is not just money or position in essence; it is the total fulfillment of my innate potential as a human being.**
9. **I shall** *enjoy whatever I do* **and finish any project within the stipulated time frame.**
10. **I am the maker of my** *own destiny* **and will give my best to be always be happy and cheerful.**

WILL

One of the easiest ways to achieve our goal is to use visible reminders. These reminders should be stuck on as many places as possible - in the home, in the office and also in our vehicles. You can create your own reminders.

It is a great idea to post these ten affirmations in your home as well, doors/windows in a room, wardrobe of the rooms or kitchen, refrigerator. These affirmations are a magical tool to sort stress!

The following are some measures which will help you de-stress instantaneously and I keep it at one statement a day. By the end of the month, I realize that the 30 different statements give me 30 different perceptions:

1. Begin, and the work will be done
2. Do it now!
3. Tomorrow never comes
4. Make today count
5. Procrastination prevents success
6. In just two days, tomorrow will be yesterday
7. Time is money
8. Do it anyway!
9. Get the now habit
10. Be a doer, not a dweller
11. Why wait?
12. Don't delay, do it now

WILL

13. Have a happy tomorrow: Do today's work today
14. If not today: WHEN?
15. Today: Use it or lose it
16. Use this day well
17. Life is leaking through your fingers
18. Do it before sundown
19. You don't find time, make it
20. Just do it!
21. Make it happen
22. Yesterday is a cancelled cheque, forget it; tomorrow is a promissory note, don't count on it; today is ready cash: use it! Due tomorrow? Do it now.
23. Well begun is half done
24. If it is worth doing, it is worth doing now
25. Move ahead or move aside
26. Winners don't wait
27. Choose this day to use this day
28. Procrastination is the thief of time
29. Do the worst first (Source: *Doing it Now* by Edwin C. Bliss)

Stress is more of how you take it, from now on call every problem as challenge and do not use the words like problem, fate, bad times, etc. words have unique power. In the way you replaced problem with challenge, change every negative word in your vocabulary. Like how you can't change your destiny, destiny can't change you either.

Action Plan for Sorting Stress

Write down the 50 likely possible scenarios, which stress you or pain you the most and write down three constructive possible solutions for this.

Chapter 5

BECOME A SINCERE AND DYNAMIC LEADER

Leadership is not about creating more followers. It is about creating more leaders.

I have explored and experienced leadership skills at both college and corporate level – colleges like St. Joesph's Bangalore, GRCIBM, rporate houses like Accenture, Infosys, etc. have taught me that each project is different. Even though at times the titles and job description may sound similar, each assignment is unique and requires a clear and fresh mind to handle.

WILL

Many years of experience and expertise in leadership have taught me that good leadership is a result of the careful application of eleven skills that any post leader or officer can learn to use. With practice, these skills can become a part of the women officer's leadership style and will prove helpful in Exploring and all other leadership situations

Understanding the Needs and Characteristics of the Post

Women make good leaders because of the inbuilt qualities of compassion, commitment and creativity. They gauge the environment in a short time, and adapt themselves to the system of the place, and see every individual team member as strategic business partner, sustainability and growth is inevitable.

Each individual member of the group has certain needs and characteristics:

1. A leader should understand her roles and responsibilities clearly because, clarity gives us the capability to perform better
2. A leader should understand the needs and characteristics of each member of the group. This helps the leader to deal with each person as an

individual, to treat that individual with respect, and to help the person grow. She should also show her subordinates the bright future and help them grow with her as well as the company.
3. This understanding helps in planning the program and in getting things done with quantified time and quality output.
4. This understanding creates trust and builds confidence among group members leading to synergy, trust and thereby enhances productivity

As a leader it is your key responsibility to understand fellow members' mindsets and set a right attitude through conversation and informal surveys members, Take an initiative to find out:

Why they joined the particular post?

What they expect from the post/programs?

What their major interests are. What is their future plan?

Always remember, plan is nothing, planning is everything.

WILL

Knowing and Using the Resources of the Group

Resources include all those things necessary to do a job. Resources also include people, because people have knowledge and skills. Knowledge is what a person learns through familiarity or experience-what you know. Skill is the ability to use what you know.

It is not about good attitude or bad attitude, it is all about the right attitude that includes the desire to do something inspiring, productive and profitable, being confident and believing that the task can be achieved

When the leader uses the knowledge and skills of group members to get a work done, the members gain experience and improve skills. They also develop a right mindset towards acquiring and using a particular skill.

Keep the learning, errors and corrections rightly documented, capability inventory up-to-date and use it in planning and application of the next project.

Increase the frequency of communication with the team. Make small agreements with the team, keep those agreements and honour those agreements.

In order to improve your skills in getting information:

Pay attention and listen carefully. Make notes and sketches. Ask questions and repeat your understanding of what was said.

To improve your skills in giving information:

Be sure others are listening before you speak. Speak slowly and clearly. Draw diagrams, if needed. Ask those receiving information, to take notes. Have the listeners repeat their understanding of what was said. Encourage questions.

Planning

Planning is an important part of everything we do in Exploring. The following is a simple process for planning:

1. Consider the task and objectives. What do you want to accomplish?
2. Consider the resources-equipment, knowledge, skills, and attitudes.
3. Consider the alternatives. Brainstorm.
4. Reach a decision, evaluating each option.
5. Write the plan down and review it with the post.
6. Execute the plan.
7. Evaluate the plan.

WILL

SYNERGY in the team builds as a result of recognizing the difference between where the group is and where the group is planning to go.

As a leader you are responsible for developing a plan to help the group get to its goal. Setting the example is the most effective way of empowering the group. When working with your team members, do the following:

Observe the group continually. Understand the situation and the attitude of the group. Make your instructions clear and pertinent. Pitch in and help when necessary – deal carefully with disruption. Guide the post toward self-discipline. Keep time cushion for delays and unexpected twists in the project.

EVALUATING the project and introspecting post project completion with the mindset of how we can continuously evolve, adds value and excellence.

Evaluating helps measure the performance of a group in getting a project done and working together facilitates ideas and where they might fit in the future projects. It suggests ways in which the group can improve its performance and break their own previous records and emerge winners. There are two basic categories of evaluation questions. After any event or activity, ask these two basic evaluation questions:

- Was the job done?
- Was the job done right?
- Was the job done on time?
- Keeping the group together and achieving the purpose.
- Were relationships between group members helped or hurt?
- Was participation equally distributed among group members?
- Did the group enjoy the activity?
- Did the group handle conflicts well?

Setting an Example

Setting an example is probably the most important leadership skill. It is the most effective way to show others the proper way to conduct themselves, and is even more effective than verbal communication. Without this skill, all the other skills would be useless. One way to think about setting the example is to imagine yourself as a member of a group and think about how you would like your leader to act.

Sharing Leadership

While there are various ways to exercise leadership, the goal of exploring leadership is exemplified in a quote from the ancient Chinese philosopher, Lao-Tzu, "But a good leader, will not only have followers, eventually followers will become leaders and create more leaders."

The exploring leader wants to give team members the skills he or she possesses, not to use those skills in ways that keep the post weak or dependent. You as a leader, offer leadership opportunities to team members and teach them the acquisition of the skills they need and makes them employable and increases their economic value.

Counseling

Counseling is important and crucial. Being a leader does not put the woman in you to inaction. We women have an innate ability to connect, correct and resolve conflict. As a leader we must help people solve problems and to encourage or to reassure. Remember, help an explorer to reach his or her potential and always remember there is a very *thin line between intruding and counseling*. Beware how much is too much.

Counseling can be effective when a person is indecisive. . Confused, i.e. he or she doesn't have enough information or has too much information. Locked in, i.e. he or she do not know any alternatives. How do you counsel?

First, try to understand the situation,

Listen carefully

Summarize

Check the facts

Repeat to make sure you understand.

Second, help list as many options as possible.

Third, help list the disadvantages of the options.

Fourth, help list the advantages of the options.

Finally, let the person decide on a solution. The counselor's role is to encourage and inform, not advice.

Representing the Group

Where do you represent the post? Post leaders represent the post at post committee meetings, advisor's meetings, officers' meetings, explorer officers' association (EOA) meetings, and planning conferences, and to the chartered organization. The leader represents the post in two situations: Without consultation - when he or she doesn't have the opportunity to consult with post officers about a decision. With consultation- when he or she can meet with post officers about the issue.

In some cases the leader must represent the post's decision exactly; in other cases, he or she must use independent judgment. You will need to solicit and analyze members' views and attempt to represent those views within the guidelines of your post, your chartered organization, and exploring the possibility of learning, leveraging by knocking down the limiting factors.

Leadership Learning & Development

This is one of the areas of extensive brainstorming while big questions remain unanswered. Who exactly is a leader?

What attributes constitute a leader?

And can you take someone who isn't a natural leader and turn them into one through continuous learning and development?

Our approach is to run programs where natural leaders can develop the skill and insight to become great ones. Leadership development or leadership training requires each and every person to be rigorous in gaining personal insight, understanding what makes them tick and stretching the boundaries of what's comfortable. Only then do we focus on the ability to see what's going on. This is the one essential quality for anyone in any position of leadership: from effectively running a company and spearheading a religious institution to nurturing a home.

Once you are able to see what is going on for others, then all the other essential leadership skills can be developed: good communication, being articulate, the ability to think on your feet, humor, flexibility, integrity, compelling presence, empathy can be continuously developed and enhanced on daily basis.

Leadership Styles and Skills

- Leadership skills are based on leadership behavior. Skills alone do not make a leader - style and behavior do. If you are interested in leadership learning and development, start with leadership behavior. Leadership is mostly about

WILL

behavior, especially towards others. People who strive for these things generally come to be regarded and respected as a leader by their people.

- Integrity - the most important requirement; without it everything else is null and void.
- Behave like a grown-up - never getting emotional with people, no shouting or ranting, even if you feel upset or angry.
- Leading by example - always put your best effort and work with determination. Help - be sure to help people when they need it.
- Fairness - treat everyone equally. Be firm and clear in dealing with bad or unethical behavior.
- Listen and understand people, make them know that you have a grasp of their condition and situation (this doesn't mean you have to agree with everyone - understanding is different to agreeing).
- Always take the responsibility and blame for your team's mistakes.
- Always give your team the credit for your successes.
- Never be a self-promoter.
- Backup and support your team.

WILL

- Be decisive, but be seen to be making fair and balanced decisions.
- Ask for your team's views, but remain neutral and objective.
- Be honest but sensitive when delivering criticism or unfavorable news.
- Always do what you say you will do - and keep your promises.
- Work hard to become expert at what you do technically, and at understanding your people's technical abilities and challenges.
- Encourage your people to grow, learn and take on as much as they want to, at a pace they can handle.
- Always accentuate the positive (say 'do it like this', not 'don't do it like that').
- Smile and encourage others to be happy and enjoy themselves.
- Relax, and give your team and yourself time to get to know and respect each other.
- Take notes and keep good records.

Plan and Prioritize

Manage your time well and help others to do so too.

Involve your people in your thinking and especially in managing change. Read great books, and take advice from wonderful people, to help develop your own understanding of yourself, and particularly of other people's weaknesses are not about business at all - they are about people who triumph over adversity. Achieve the company tasks and objectives, but never at the cost of your integrity or the trust of your people.

Exploring Leadership Skills

Many years of experience in exploration have shown that good leadership is a result of the careful application of eleven skills that any post leader or officer can learn to use. With practice, these skills can become a part of the adult's or young officer's leadership style and will prove helpful in exploring and all other leadership situations.

Leadership Development Guidelines

While leadership is easy to explain, leadership is not so easy to practice. Leadership is about behavior first, skills second. Good leaders are followed chiefly because people trust and respect them, rather than the skills they possess. Leadership is different to management.

WILL

Management relies more on planning, organizational and communications skills. Leadership relies on management skills too, but more so on qualities such as integrity, honesty, humility, courage, commitment, sincerity, passion, confidence, positive thinking, wisdom, determination, compassion and sensitivity. Some people are born to be natural leaders than others. Most people don't seek to be a leader. Those who want to be a leader can develop leadership ability. Leadership can be performed with different styles. Some leaders have one style, which is right for certain situations and wrong for others. Some leaders can adapt and use different leadership styles for given situations.

Tips on Leadership

There is only one way - the strategic way. It sets the tone of the organization. Be open to the best of what everyone, everywhere, has to offer. You should transfer learning across your organization.

1. Get the right people in the right jobs - is more important than developing a strategy.
2. An informal atmosphere has a competitive advantage.

WILL

3. Ensure everybody counts and everybody knows that they count.
4. Self Confidence is power, the true test of self confidence is the courage to be open.
5. Business has to be fun - celebrations energize and organization.
6. Never underestimate the other person.
7. Understand where real value is added and put your best people there.
8. Be aware when to meddle and when to let go - this is pure instinct.
9. As a leader, your main priority is to get the job done, whatever the job is. Leaders make things happen by:
10. Knowing your objectives and having a plan to achieve them.

Building a team committed to achieving the objectives.

Helping each team member to give his or her best effort.

Introspect on Self, Dig for Gold in Others

As a leader you must know yourself. Know your strengths and weaknesses, so that you can build the best team around you. Communication is critical. Listen, consult, involve, and explain why as well as what needs to be done. Some leaders lead by example and are very 'hands on'; others are more distanced and let their people do it. Whatever is the method, your example is paramount - the way you work and conduct yourself will be the most you can possibly expect from your people. If you set low standards you are to blame for low standards in your people.

Praise loudly, blame softly.

– Catherine the Great

Follow this maxim.

Take time to listen to and really understand people. Walk the job. Ask and learn about what people do and think, and how they think improvements can be made.

Emphasize the positive. Express things in terms of what should be done, and never about what should not be done. If you emphasize the negative, people are more likely to veer towards it. Like the mother who left her five-year-old for a minute unsupervised in the kitchen, saying as she left the room, "...don't you go putting those beans up your nose." We know what must have followed.

Take difficult decisions bravely, and be truthful and sensitive when you implement them.

Constantly seek to learn from the people around you - they will teach you more about yourself than anything else. They will also tell you 90% of what you need to know to achieve your business goals.

Embrace the change, but not for change's sake. Change before change changes you. Begin to plan your the succession as soon as you take up your new post, and in this regard, ensure that the only promises you should ever make are those that you can guarantee to deliver.

Concepts of Leadership

Good leaders are made, not born. If you have the desire and willpower, you can become an effective leader. Good leaders develop through a never-ending process of self-study, education, training, and experience. This guide will help you to understand that process.

To inspire your workers into higher levels of teamwork, there are certain things you must be, know, and, do.

WILL

These do not come naturally, but are acquired through continuous work and study. Good leaders continually work and study to improve their leadership skills; they do not rest on their laurels.

People can choose to become leaders. People can learn leadership skills. This is the Transformational Leadership Theory. It is the most widely accepted theory today and the premise on which this guide is based. When a person takes you to be his/her leader, he/she do not think about your attributes, rather, he/she observe what you do so that he/she can know who you really are. She uses this observation to tell if you are a honorable and trusted leader or a self serving person who misuses authority to look good and get promoted. Self-serving leaders are not as effective because their employees only obey them, not follow them. They succeed in many areas because they present a good image to their seniors at the expense of their workers.

The basis of good leadership is honorable character and selfless service to your organization. In your employees' eyes, your leadership is everything you do that affects the organization's objectives and their well-being. Respected leaders concentrate on what they are (such as beliefs and character), what they know (such as job, tasks, and human nature), and what they do (such as implementing, motivating, and provide direction).

What makes a person want to follow a leader? People want to be guided by those they respect and who have a clear sense of direction. To gain respect, one must be ethical. A sense of direction is achieved by conveying a strong vision of the future.

The Two Most Important Keys to Effective Leadership

Hay's study examined over 75 key components of employee satisfaction. They found that, trust and confidence in top leadership was the single most reliable predictor of employee satisfaction in an organization. Effective communication by leadership in three critical areas was the key to winning organizational trust and confidence. The three critical areas are as follows:

Helping employees understand how they contribute to achieving key business objectives.

Sharing information with employees on both how the company is doing and how an employee's own division is doing - relative to strategic business objectives.

WILL

Helping and sharing will have no relevance if one is not trustworthy. Trust builds the platform to gain support. It promotes helping, sharing and caring. This is the third and most critical area for being an effective leader.

So in a nutshell, you must be trustworthy and you have to be able to communicate a vision of where the organization needs to go. The next section, "Principles of Leadership," is close to this key concept.

Principles of Leadership

To help you be, know, do and have; (U.S. Army, 1973) follow these eleven principles of leadership:

Know yourself and seek self-improvement - In order to know yourself, you have to understand your being, knowing, doing and having attributes. Seeking self-improvement simply means continually strengthening your attributes and giving your in everything you do for self, business or life.

This can be accomplished through self-study, formal classes, reflection, and interacting with others.

WILL

Be technically proficient: As a leader, you must know your job and have a solid familiarity with your employees' tasks.

Seek responsibility and take responsibility for your actions: Search for ways to guide your organization to new heights. And when things go wrong, they always do sooner or later -do not blame others. Analyze the situation, take corrective action, and move on to the next challenge.

Make sound and timely decisions - Use good problem solving, decision-making, and planning tools.

Know your people and look out for their well-being - Know human nature and the importance of sincerely caring for your workers.

Ensure that tasks are understood, supervised, and accomplished - Communication is the key to this responsibility.

Train as a team - Although many so called leaders call their organization, department, section, etc. a team; they are not really teams, they are just a group of people doing their jobs.

Factors of Leadership

There are four major factors in leadership, they are:

1. Follower
2. Leader
3. Communication
4. Situation

Follower

Different people require different styles of leadership. For example, a new hire requires more supervision than an experienced employee. A person who lacks motivation requires a different approach than one with a greater motivation. You must know your people and how to inspire them so as to bring out the best in them. The fundamental starting point is to have a good understanding of human nature, such as needs, emotions, and motivation. You must become to know your employees' be, know, and do attributes.

Leader

You must have an honest understanding of yourself in terms of who you are, what you know, and what you can do. Also, note that it is the followers, not the leader who determines if a leader is successful. If the followers do not trust or lack confidence in their leader, then they will be uninspired. To be successful you have to convince your followers, not yourself or your superiors, that you are worthy of being followed.

Communication

You have to establish two-way communication. Much of it is nonverbal. For instance, when you "set an example," it communicates to your people that you would not ask them to perform anything that you would not be willing to do. What and how you communicate either builds or harms the relationship between you and your employees.

Situation

<u>All situations are </u>different. What you do in one situation will not always work in another. You must use your judgment to decide the best course of action and the leadership style needed for each situation. For example, you may need to confront an employee for inappropriate behavior, but if the confrontation is too late or too early, too harsh or too weak, then the results may prove ineffective.

WILL

Various forces will affect these factors. Examples of such forces are your relationship with your seniors, the skill of your people, the informal leaders within your organization, and how your company is organized.

Attributes

If you are a leader who can be trusted, then those around you will grow to respect you. To be such a leader, there is a Leadership Framework to guide you.

Environment

Every organization has a particular work environment, which dictates, to a considerable degree, how its leaders respond to problems and opportunities. This is brought about by its heritage of past leaders and its present leaders.

Goals, Values and Concepts

Leaders exert influence on the environment via three types of actions: a) The goals and performance standards they establish. b) The values they establish for the organization. c) The business and people concepts they establish.

WILL

Successful organizations have leaders who set high standards and goals across the entire spectrum, such as strategies, market leadership, plans, meetings and presentations, productivity, quality, and reliability. Values reflect the organization's concern for its employees, customers, investors, vendors, and neighboring community. These values define the manner in which the business will be conducted.

Concepts define what products or services the organization will offer and the methods and processes for conducting business. These goals, values, and concepts make up the organization's "personality" or how do both outsiders and insiders observe the organization. This personality defines the roles, relationships, rewards, and rites that take place.

Leadership Models

Leadership models help us to understand what makes leaders act the way they do. The ideal is not to restrict yourself to a type of behavior discussed in the model, but to realize that every situation calls for a different approach or behavior to be taken. Two models will be discussed, the Four Framework Approach and the Managerial Grid.

Four Framework Approach

In the Four Framework Approach, Bolman and Deal (1991) suggest that leaders display leadership behaviors in one of four types of frameworks: *Structural, Human Resource, Political, or Symbolic*. The style can either be either effective or ineffective, depending upon the chosen behavior. *Structural Framework*

In an effective leadership situation, the leader is a social architect whose leadership style is analysis and design. While in an ineffective leadership situation, the leader is a petty tyrant whose leadership style is details. Structural leaders focus on structure, strategy, environment, implementation, experimentation, and adaptation.

Human Resource Framework

In an effective leadership situation, the leader is a catalyst and servant whose leadership style is to support, advocate, and empower. While in an ineffective leadership situation, the leader is a pushover, whose leadership style is abdication and fraud. Human Resource leaders believe in people and communicate that belief; they are visible and accessible; they empower, increase participation, support, share information, and move decision-making down into the organization.

Political Framework

In an effective leadership situation, the leader is an advocate, whose leadership style is to sustain growth and be in sync with the team. While in an ineffective leadership situation, the leader is a hustler, whose leadership style is manipulation. Political leaders clarify what they want and what they can get they assess the distribution of power and interests; they build links to other stakeholders, use persuasion first, then use negotiation and coercion only if necessary.

Symbolic Framework

In an effective leadership situation, the leader is a prophet, whose leadership style is inspirational. While in an ineffective leadership situation, the leader is a fanatic or fool, whose leadership style is smoke and mirrors. Symbolic leaders view organizations as a stage or theater to play certain roles and give impressions; these leaders use symbols to capture attention; they try to frame experience by providing plausible interpretations of experiences; they discover and communicate a vision.

The Four Framework Approach suggests that leaders can be put into one of these four categories and there are times when one approach is appropriate and times when it is not.. Any one of these approaches alone would be inadequate, thus we should strive to be conscious of all four approaches, and not only on one or two approaches. For example, during a major organizational change, a structural leadership style may be more effective than a visionary leadership style; while during a period when strong growth is needed, the visionary approach may be better. We also need to be aware of ourselves, as each of us tends to have a preferred approach.

Types of Leaders

The world has seen many types of leaders. A leadership style is exclusively based on the personality of the leader.

Indira Gandhi was Prime Minister of India for almost 17 years. All that matters is, was she effective? If yes, what type of leadership style did she follow?

Authoritarian Leader

(High task, low relationship) People who get this rating are task oriented and are hard on their workers (autocratic). There is little or no allowance for cooperation or collaboration. Heavily task oriented people display these characteristics: they are very firm about schedules; they expect people to do what they are told without question or debate; when something goes wrong they tend to focus on who is to blame rather than concentrate on what exactly is wrong and how to prevent further it; they are intolerant of what they see as dissent (it may just be someone's creativity), so it is difficult for their subordinates to contribute or develop.

Team Leader

(High task, high relationship) This type of person leads by positive example and endeavors to foster a team environment in which all team members can reach their highest potential, both as team members and as people. They encourage the team to reach team goals as effectively as possible, while also working tirelessly to strengthen the bonds among the various members. They normally form and lead some of the most productive teams.

Country Club Leader

These leaders predominantly reward power to maintain discipline and to encourage the team to accomplish the goals. Conversely, they are almost incapable of employing the more punitive coercive and legitimate powers. This inability results from fear that using such powers could jeopardize relationships with the other team members.

Impoverished Leader

(Low task, low relationship) This is a leader who uses a "delegate and disappear" management style. Since they are not committed to either task accomplishment or maintenance; they essentially allow their team to do whatever it wishes and prefer to detach themselves from the team process by allowing the team to suffer a series of power struggles.

The Process of Great Leadership

The road to great leadership that is common to successful leaders:

Challenge the process - first, find a process that you believe needs to be improved the most.

Inspire a shared vision - next, share you vision in words that can be understood by your followers.

Enable others to act - give them the tools and methods to solve the problem.

Model the way - when the process gets tough, get your hands dirty. A boss tells others what to do, a leader shows that it can be done.

Encourage the heart - share the glory with your followers, while keeping the pains within your own.

Leadership and Human Behavior

Human needs are an important part of human nature. Values, beliefs, and customs differ from country to country and group to group, but all people have similar needs. As a leader you must understand these needs because they are powerful motivators.

Maslow felt that human needs were arranged in a hierarchical order. He based his theory on healthy, creative people who used all their talents, potential, and capabilities. At the time, this methodology differed from most other psychological research studies, in that they were based on observing disturbed people. As a leader, you need to interact with your followers, peers, seniors, and others, whose support you need in order to accomplish your objectives. To gain their support, you must be able to understand and motivate them. To understand and motivate people, you must know human nature. Human nature is the common qualities of all human beings. People behave according to certain principles of human nature. These principles govern our behavior.

A need higher in the hierarchy will become a motive of behavior as long as the needs below it have been satisfied. Unsatisfied lower needs will dominate unsatisfied higher needs and must be satisfied before the person can climb up the hierarchy.

Knowing where a person is located on this scale aids in determining an effective motivator. For example, motivating a middle-class person (who is in range 4 of the hierarchy) with a certificate will have a far greater impact of motivation than using the same motivator to affect a minimum wage person from the ghetto who is desperately struggling to meet the first couple of needs.

It should be noted that almost no one stays in one particular hierarchy for an extended period. We

WILL

constantly strive to move up, while at the same time various forces outside our control try to push us down.

Those on top get pushed down for short time periods, i.e. death of a loved-one or an idea that does not work, while those on the bottom get pushed up, i.e., come across a small prize. Our goal as leaders therefore is to help people obtain the skills and knowledge that will push them up the hierarchy on a more permanent basis. People who have their basic needs met become much better workers as they are able to concentrate on fulfilling the visions put forth to them, rather than consistently struggling to make ends meet.

If I had to summarize leadership in a statement, I would say:

Lead effectively or bleed sufficiently.

If your presence cannot make any impact, your absence will not make any difference. Don't worry about being a perfect leader, worry if you are not a progressive leader.

Chapter 6

BECOME A STORYTELLER AND AN EFFECTIVE COMMUNICATOR

Effective Communication

Effective Communication is the art of imparting or conveying ideas, views or information from one person to another. Being an expert in this subject imparting effective communication in various forums, associations and colleges, I have realized effective communication is an intercourse of words, letters, symbols or messages to create an impact; and is a way that one organization/family member shares meaning and understanding with another. Communication is a two-way operation that involves sending and receiving signals. Empowered communicators learn to receive signals so they can be proactive rather than be reactive to what they send. When the bonding in the team is strong you can be assured they share healthy and clear communication. Be it personal or professional, if there is no communication barrier and the thought process flows effectively - you can expect successful relationships and organizations.

When communicating, step into the shoes of the other person. Read the body language, tone of voice, statements, and also the silence. Investigate the other person's motivation and fear. Don't take communication for granted. It is not only the right attitude, but also an acquired skill - a fantastic technique to convey your message, an amazing art to foster relationships, a facility of elevating expression and thereby bringing success.

Parts of Communication

In any situation or scenario, this is the makeup of communication:

Speaking - 30%

Listening - 45%
Reading - 16%
Writing - 9%

Improving Communication the Godwin Way

At the GODWIN workshops communication is not taught. It is drilled into participants. The participants are encouraged to do the following things through knowledge sharing, group discussions, brainstorming activities, team tasks and experiential games:

a. Playing games is the reflection of behavior in real life.
b. Interacting frequently leads to cooperation at all levels.
c. Effective listening promotes collaborative ideas.
d. Showing slides enhances graphical visualization.
e. Exhibiting videos guides the imageries of the mind.
f. Making the participants speak helps in building bonds and makes communication flow smoothly.
g. Assigning judgmental roles help them prepare for the leadership roles.

How does Communication Help?

- *It helps us to interact with someone, create an impression and make an impact.*
- *It helps others to interact with us and assits in understanding.*
- *It satisfies a need for problem solving – for conflict resolving and fosters better relationship.*
- *It satisfies our ego and reduces 'I know it all' attitude.*
- *It satisfies our need for recognition, status and belonging.*
- *It helps to release our tension, fear and anxiety and builds camaraderie. It satisfies a great desire of every human being to acquire warmth and affection from another person and this contributes to team strength.*

The Need for Better Communication

A woman is a fantastic communicator. As a social being she always relates to situations and scenarios, a quality that comes from her very nature. Communication is so interwoven in our daily lives that few people realize how much time is devoted to it. The better we identify the need of communication, the better we communicate.

Though we are urged to hold on to being individual, separate, distinct and different from our gentlemen, yet we are urged to be with them, to relate with them and to love and be loved and accepted by them. Hence, being an effective communicator is worth more than money can buy.

Psychology of Communication

Communication is relationship with people. It is psychological, for no individual's actions prove him or her human as much as communication. It tells of the person and reveals the person. Human beings are communicative and linguistic. In principle, at least, they are able to communicate signs with other human beings. He is able to establish a relationship a relationship that implies the use of his body and psychological faculties of mind and will. The psychology of communication, therefore is concerned with the behavior and attitude of man as communicator, for psychology attempts to study and describe mental and behavioral events in man. Of course, it is not limited to talking or listening. Other kinds of messages or events, intentional or unintentional, can also serve the purpose of communication.

WILL

Impossible Communication

It is impossible to communicate effectively if you: a)Neglect to listen to what the other person is saying b) Stubbornly refuse to see another point of view c) Refuse to accept that others are entitled to their views and opinions d) Over-react to others comments and views.

When we are urging to be treated as equals in the society, an era in which are not competing with the gentlemen, but with ourselves, we should exercise caution that we should not claim or take stance with gender privilege at the time of crisis and distress.

Never use the defensive layer of our nature - being emotional or becoming teary eyed during the challenging times or seeking concession in the penalty for being faulty. We are accountable for our deeds and action.

Important in Communication

Make sure to remember these points when communicating:

- Don't try to communicate when you are angry.
- Avoid arguments and criticizing others.

- Always answer a question directly and then explain.
- Precede questions with necessary information.
- Make your point early.
- Be clear about the scope of your subject.
- Repeat yourself to get your point across.
- Try to get a response from your listener .
- Ask for your listeners' opinion when you sense disagreement.

Barriers to Communication

- Message is vague in sender's mind.
- Failing to understand receiver's background and perception.
- Failing to define message properly.
- Attributing blame or imposing guilt.
- Threatening or attacking another's self esteem.
- Using jargon, acronyms or technical language.
- Gaming: Attempting to manipulate or control receiver by confusing or obscuring message.

The Process of Communication

The communication process consists of three elements:

- The sender
- The medium by which the signal is sent
- The receiver

Communication is a basic element to establish a communion with someone. Its process implies a series of actions or components.

They are: Source - Encoder / Speaker - Signal / Message – Decoder - Destination / Receiver - Feedback.

Effective Communication

Effective communication requires not merely the transmission of information but also the sharing of a message; not only the sharing of a message, but also sharing of the meaning of the message; not only sharing of the meaning of the message, but also the sharing of life itself – which is communion.

Types of Communication

- Intrapersonal
- Interpersonal
- Verbal
- Non-verbal
- Written

- Group
- Mass
- Persuasive
- Business

Intrapersonal

A communication begins with the self, with the communication that goes on within the self, in the intrapersonal communication. It is the basis of all communication with others. Before we understand the communication with others, we must first understand how we communicate within ourselves, for we always communicate who we are and what we are much more than we communicate information.

Interpersonal

We live and work in a society that values communication. The society cannot go on unless its members communicate with one another, and interact one another. We need interpersonal communication, that is, the communication among persons. It operates at every level of relationship:

1. one-to-one,
2. one-to-two,

3. one-to-many

'People skills' is an important aspect of any job. Today, more than ever, managerial success depends on how well you relate to your team. What you say is often not important as how you say it. Influencing others and ensuring the message you sent was received, as intended is vitally important.

Verbal

The intercourse of human interchange is handled mainly through language. He who ignores the mastery of skills in language will ignore in every other effective attribute. Language is psychological, poetical and social. It has psychological value because through it our knowledge becomes clearer, more distinct and easier. People, who have deeper insight, think in wider horizon. The social value lies in this that through language social life is strengthened. Language molds the society.

Improvement in communication is clarity between what we mean to say and what we say means. It is important that the talker and the listener have the same frame of mind.

WILL

Nonverbal

Human Language is the medium through which we share and reveal certain information about ourselves.

There are two main types of communication: Symbolic and Empathic.

Symbolic - Symbolic communication consists of spoken or written language, signs and gestures. It covers such vastly different things as; mathematics, instruments panels, scoreboards, signal lights, secret codes and so on.

Empathic - Empathic communication is nonverbal. It is more of an exchange of feelings. We cannot ignore or belittle its importance because the greater part of our communication is consists of unspoken feelings and emotions.

Everything is a sign of communication - According to some theoreticians; there is no sharp line between the means of communication and the external world. All exists through interaction like the atom.

Mineralogy, biology and zoology give attention to the system of interaction within minerals, organisms and so on, and the interaction between them and the milieu.

Touch - The physical body is the bridge, which connects our inner and outer worlds. In a sense, it carries a two-way traffic. First, it brings the outer world in through the wonder of the physical senses.

Second, it enables us to project our inner ideas and visions outward into reality, thereby changing the world around us.

Clothes - Clothes carry a message both for the wearer and the viewer. They affect our personality and consequently our behavior. Your clothes, your hair style, your shoes, your way of standing, sitting and walking, your way of working, are all ways of communicating.

Dance - In dancing, communication is poetry and music. Dance energizes the body, spiritualizing the soul. It requires accuracy both in movements and in words.

Example - Examples are a most efficacious means of communication, by far more efficacious than precepts, and worth a thousand arguments.

Sports - Sports is a means of nonverbal communication. It is a means to express oneself. A sportsman said 'to me sport is a search for a means of communication. I truly get satisfaction from it.

Music - Music is an art and a great means of communication. It is well said to be the speech of angels. It certainly helps to make life happier and healthier.

Sensitive to Signals - To be aware of the many signs, signals, an essential function of communication is to be alive and sensitive to the most basic human need.

In our day-to-day communication, you and I tend to treat both people and objects in the same way. We rarely treat them as exclusively one way or the other, but when treat them as objects, we don't allow interpersonal communication to happen, and when we are treating them primarily as humans, we are.

Written

Even if you have to apply for a job, the person interviewing you will ask for a written resume. If you send one by e-mail, he will surely take a printout and have it with him or else he will ask you for a hard copy of the resume. Such is the importance of written communication.

WILL

The language today is more audiovisual. People get most of their information through sight and sound. Nevertheless, the printed word is still considered the first and undoubtedly most important among the media of communication. To inform, to entertain and to convince, you need more than clarity. You need style, flair, and integrity of words and action. These characteristics can be easily achieved by writing your message, for your own benefit and, if you care, about your listeners or readers.

Group

People in a group interact with one another. They have some cohesive bond and have a purpose, defined or not. They meet to discuss or talk about a common topic, to inform about himself or herself or some other business. In a group communication, everyone has something to contribute, for we are all unique. People, who casually meet in a lift or in a market place, do not form a group.

Mass

One of the most interesting and significant developments that we are witnessing today is in the realm of mass communication. It is the communication which uses technical media like television, radio, cinema, newspapers, books, video-cassettes, compact discs, internet and the like. The mass communication is oriented to a vast number of persons who are not contacted personally. Perhaps the media that have still the largest possible reach and penetration is the radio. However TV is recognized as the most powerful vehicle for dissemination of education, information, culture and entertainment.

The means of mass communication – mass media, in spite of many drawbacks, unite different countries and regions of the world despite great geographical distances. They are made to realize that all countries and all people have to live in an essentially interdependent world.

Persuasive

Whether you are a public speaker or are talking at home, in the office, in the factory or among friends, your talk should be plain, clear and persuasive, if you would like to be listened to. Beyond listening, communication also means getting your ideas across to others. Communication is not only what you say, but how you say it. When a human action is both indispensable and difficult, it ordinarily requires preliminary, conditions, readiness. It is more than remotely possible that we fail in communication because we are not prepared. If we do not know ourselves or if we are not ready to communicate person to person we will have difficulty in communicating.

Business Communication

Business communication is a means of communication like any other. The only difference is that we need certain skills to conduct business smoothly and most importantly successfully. We cannot have a person with low energy to manage the front office in a service industry, The client who walks in also will rub on to the low energy levels. That reminds me of a certain funny situation, when I was heading one of India's leading express companies. A certain field staff was entrusted with the task of attending to call after office hours. A qualified receptionist was manning the counter till about 6.00 pm. One day the staff attended a call at 7.00 pm and responded, "Good Night! Launch Pad Couriers!" The man on the other side went bonkers. He hung up. A few days later when my sales executive went there to see him he just said a few words, 'If your people do not know how to talk I am sure you would do the same with my parcels' we lost that customer all because of the 'Good night!'

Hence the point home that business communication needs to be addressed very seriously by any organization which needs to stay in the market.

Effective Listening Skills

Communication is a two-way process- without effective listening there can be no effective communication. Listening goes with the presence of mind and your concentration levels. There are occasions where a person tells his name and introduces himself. At that moment your mind is wandering and something else is playing in your mind, maybe the color of his shirt or for that matter his visage which may be familiar and so on. You do not register it.

The same holds for the students who are in a class or even a person who is in a workshop. Listening is important so is what the others say. "Listen to what I say" is a very common phrase which people use. That means the other person wants your attention. Listening is a learned skill. Don't undervalue the ability to listen.

Public Speaking

My experience as a lecturer, at GRCIBM imparting Effective Communication to students, who had to complete it as a course title as a part of completion of their three years Diploma in Business Administration at SJP Campus is unforgettable. I enjoy myself more whenever I handle sessions; this session was particularly unforgettable as I taught in the same college where I studied, because most of them were unaware of communication basics. This particular session which I am about to talk about was on Public Speaking where a topic was given and the participant had to speak on it for two minutes.

The time given for preparation was about three minutes. After the preparation time instructions read out the participants, who were 25 in number, came up on stage and were asked to talk. Instructions were given to participants to stand within the circle and move about as they speak. There were three (Sara, Seema & Savitha) outstanding participants whose experiences I would like to share with you. Sara came up and stood like a statue all through the two minutes of her speech. Evaluation was done.

WILL

Then came Seema who took too much liberty and began moving like a cat in a cage. She began circling round and round and moved her hands too much. Evaluation was done. Then came Savitha. She took a clue from both Sara and Seema and neither stood like a statue nor paced like a cat. Her talk was balanced and finally she got the best opinion. We have to emulate Savitha to be a good public speaker.

Here's What You Need to Know

Speak with conviction as if you really believe in what you are saying.

- Persuade your audience effectively.
- Do not read from notes for any extended length of time although it is quite acceptable to glance at your notes infrequently.
- Speak loudly and clearly. Sound confident. Do not mumble. If you made an error, correct it, and continue. No need to make excuses or apologize profusely.
- Maintain sincere eye contact with your audience.
- Use the three-second method, e.g. look straight into the eyes of a person in the audience for three seconds at a time.

WILL

- Have direct eye contact with a number of people in the audience, and every now and then glance at the whole audience while speaking. Use your eye contact to make everyone in your audience feel involved.
- Speak to your audience, listen to their questions, respond to their reactions, adjust, adapt and appreciate.
- Pause. Allow yourself and your audience a little time to reflect and think. Don't race through your presentation and leave your audience, as well as yourself, feeling out of breath.
- Add humor whenever appropriate and possible. Keep audience interested throughout your entire presentation.
- Remember that an interesting speech makes time fly, but a boring speech is always too long to endure even if the presentation time is the same.
- When using audio-visual aids to enhance your presentation, be sure all necessary equipment is set up and in good working order prior to the presentation.
- Have handouts ready and give them out at the appropriate time.
- Know when to stop talking.

WILL

Top Nine Tips for Public Speaking

Feeling some nervousness before giving a speech is natural and healthy. It shows you care about doing well. But, too much nervousness can be detrimental. Here's how you can control your nervousness and make effective, memorable presentations:

1. Know the room. Be familiar with the place in which you will speak. Arrive early, walk around the speaking area and practice using the microphone and any visual aids.
2. Know the audience. Greet some of the audience as they arrive. It's easier to speak to a group of friends than to a group of strangers.
3. Know your material. If you're not familiar with your material or are uncomfortable with it, your nervousness will increase. Practice your speech and revise it if necessary.
4. Relax. Ease tension by doing exercises.
5. Visualize yourself giving the speech. Imagine yourself speaking, your voice loud, clear, and assured. When you visualize yourself as successful, you will be successful.
6. Realize that people want you to succeed. Audiences want you to be interesting,

stimulating, informative, and entertaining. They don't want you to fail.

7. Don't apologize. If you mention your nervousness or apologize for any problems you think you have with your speech, you may be calling the audience's attention to something they hadn't noticed. Keep silent.
8. Concentrate on the message - not the medium. Focus your attention away from your own anxieties, and outwardly toward your message and your audience. Your nervousness will dissipate. Turn nervousness into positive energy. Harness your nervous energy and transform it into vitality and enthusiasm.
9. Gain experience. Experience builds confidence, which is the key to effective speaking.

Body Language

Body language is the unspoken communication that goes on in every face-to-face encounter with another human being. It tells you their true feelings towards you and how well your words are being received. About 60-80% of our messages are communicated through our conscious and unconscious movements. Only about 7%-10% is attributable to the actual words of a conversation. Your ability to read and understand another person's body language can mean the difference between making a great impression or a very bad one. It could help you in that job interview, that meeting, that business function, or special date!

Every one of us has experienced that feeling of an instant like or dislike of someone, without necessarily knowing why. We just weren't happy, there was something about them. We often refer to this as a hunch or gut feeling, two descriptions directly relating to our own body's physiological reaction.

Power of Words

What you say is also just as important. Words like arrows, once out of the mouth, nothing in this world can stop them from creating havoc or happiness in the other person's mind. Your choice of words reflects your personality and maturity. You can use words to generate optimism, and motivate people or push them to depths of despair.

Do not say anything that you will not put on paper and sign. Always use words that create positive effect or neutral expression with others. The tone of your voice, if

WILL

not carefully monitored, can be a turnoff to others. You might convey a totally different impression compared to your statements if the tone does not match the situation and words.

Chapter 7

MIND AND MEMORY MANAGEMENT

Our mind plays a vital role in our capacity to impact love and leadership, our mind if set to systems and trained in memory can do wonders.

Mind Dynamics will help a woman to become extraordinary in expressing her thoughts, deeds and action.

Mind can execute any command if given with conviction and train them take orders. Make the most of your dynamic mind & memory.

WILL

1. It was finally realized that the center of thought and consciousness was located in the head, but the brain remained a mystery.
2. The average brain is far more capable than we ever believed.
3. Electrochemical interactions continually take place in our brain
4. Each side of our brain controls the opposite side of our body.
5. Left brain handles, mathematics, language, logic, analysis, writing, etc.
6. Right side handles, imagination, color, music, rhythm, daydreaming, etc.
7. Robert Evan Ornstein, an American psychologist found that when the "weaker" of the two brains was stimulated and encouraged to work in cooperation with the stronger side, the end result was a great increase in overall ability and effectiveness.

When one side was "added" to the other side, the result was often five to ten times more effective.

1. Einstein, for instance, considered to be the greatest scientist of his time, was not simply a fuzzy-headed mathematical physicist whose brain

was full of numbers and formulae. Records show that he failed in mathematics at school and that he was nearly thrown out of college for daydreaming. According to Einstein himself, he discovered his theory of relativity not seated in front of his desk, but while lying on a hill one summer day.

2. Famous painters as Klee, Cézanne and Picasso were exceptionally good in mathematical and geometrical descriptions of what they are trying to do, outlining in intricate detail the specific interrelationships they are trying to make with color, form and line.

3. Many investigations showed that great minds have been mistakenly labeled either as "artistic" or as "scientific" when in fact they were both.

4. One of the greatest brains of all time: Leonardo da Vinci, excelled in his mathematical, linguistic, logical and analytical faculties, while excelling in his ability to use imagination, color, rhythm and form.

5. Each one of us has the potential to be both exceptionally scientific and artistic.

6. Brain is composed of many thousands of intricate nerve and blood pathways. Each brain is composed of millions of tiny cells called neurons.

WILL

Each brain cell is like a tiny octopus, having a center, or a nucleus, and a large number of little tentacles radiating in all directions from it. An average brain contains a staggering number of individual neurons: 10,000 million. The number of brain cells determined the comparative intelligence of the person, but this belief was soon laid to rest when it was found that many people with "large" brains were unintelligent, whereas a number of people with "small" brains showed considerable intelligence. In the last year of his life, Professor Anokin calculated the number of connections and pathways that could be made by a normal brain. He emphasized, as a scientist, that his estimate was conservative, and concluded his last public statement by saying that he was convinced that no man was alive or had ever lived who had even approached the full use of his brain.

7. The number of connections and pathways that neurons can make is still staggering: 1 followed by 10 million kilometers of standard type written noughts.

8. The brain is much better than it has been given credit for, and most of the problems that we experience with the use of our brains are not

because of any fundamental inability but because we have so far not received enough information about ourselves and the way we work.

9. In the light of all this, the old contention that we lose brain cells continually throughout our lives and that this causes serious mental decline *fades into insignificance.* Apart from the fact that we can generate new connections far more rapidly than the average loss of brain cells, it can also be shown that even if we lose 10,000 brain cells a day from the time we are born, we have started with so many that the total number lost by the age of 80 would be less than 3%.

10. It has been calculated, for instance, that the entire network of the world's telephone systems, if properly compared to your brain, would occupy a part of the size of an ordinary garden pea.

11. It has also been discovered by Professor D. Samuel of the Weizmann Institute in Israel that at any given moment there are between 100,000 and a million chemical reactions taking place in our brain.

12. Human brain is a biological supercomputer.

WILL

How Our Mind Works

1. Our brain's primary function is to protect us from harm and ensure that everything in our body is working as it should do. The brain is responsible for maintaining our body in a state called homeostasis, in which it can sustain all the chemical processes which contribute keeping you alive. Its capacity for receiving, storing and acting on information, however, would not in itself be enough to ensure homeostasis unless it could also coordinate all our systems so that they work together rather than against each other.
2. All our life-support systems are closely linked, and dependent on each other. We could not digest and use food, for example, without a circulatory system that absorbed and distributed nutrients around the body.

It is the brain that ensures that all these actions start happening at just the right moment. The result is that we make no unnecessary movements, and our body starts producing enzymes (the chemicals that help us digest our food) only when they are needed. If all these activities are not coordinated, food might pass right through our digestive system without being broken down into a form the body could use, even if it managed to get into the right places to begin with.

Basic Principles of Memory

If you want to develop extraordinary memory, you should bear in mind the following aspects.

Your real possession is your memory. Everything you do is based on memory. The mind is like a hard disc of a computer which can accommodate any amount of information. But hard disc has its limitation but not the mind.

All knowledge is but remembrance. THERE IS NO LIMIT TO THE CAPACITY OF OUR MEMORY. The more you remember, the more you can remember, therefore, keep in mind there is no such thing as too big a memory system. Experience is your reaction to the stimuli.

There is no such thing as ultimate forgetting. Traces once impressed upon the memory are indelible and indestructible. For example, take a glass of water. Put into it a chalk piece. It gets dissolved in course of time. Though it is not visible its impact is there. Same is the case with all our experiences. We exercise our muscles and limbs. Similarly, memory has to be exercised.

WILL

The capacity for memory differs from person to person. Through training, this can be definitely improved. When you get training on memory your capacity to memorize and reproduce will improve. The true art of memorizing is the art of attention. Memory and observation go hand in hand. You can't remember anything you do not observe. The eyes cannot see if the mind is absent. It is extremely difficult to observe or remember anything that you do not want to remember. Therefore, interest and motivation are essential requisites for a good memory.

You should trust your capacity for memorizing. The more you trust it, the more reliable and useful it becomes. When you try to write down everything without any attempt to remember you do not trust your memory. You have not the confidence in your memory. There is no such thing as a good memory for one thing and bad memory for another thing. It is a question of your interest. If you are interested, you can remember anything you want.

Training in Memory

You are able to absorb more when anything is done with full concentration.

WILL

Your absorption capacity is greater when the mind reaches Alpha Waves of mental state. Therefore, before studying any book or any other material, bring the mind to alpha level.

Application of the principle of "Aware and Beware" will remove absent-mindedness.

Daily practice your memory filing technique without fail. Recollecting memory files can be treated as a meditational technique.

If it is possible you may go beyond 100 files. With the expansion of memory files, you can do wonders and marvels in the field of memory.

Imagination and creative thinking form part of a strong system of memory. Therefore, develop the faculty of creative thinking.

Every day try to memorize 100 digit numbers as a matter of practice and this will improve your capacity for concentration to a considerable extent, in addition to developing willpower, self-control and confidence in your mental ability.

WILL

How does One Develop Good Memory?

- The mental block that "my memory is poor" should be eliminated. There is no limit to the capacity of memory, the more you remember, still more you can remember.
- There is no such thing as bad and good memory. It is only trained and untrained memory.
- Everyone can develop his capacity to memorize through Memory Filing System.
- Interest and motivation are essential requisites for good memory.
- Memory improves with concentration.
- Absorption capacity is greater when the mind is at Alpha level.
- Practice daily the Memory Filing Technique- This can constitute meditational technique.
- Memory Filing System will also improve imagination and creativity.
- Try to memorize 100 digit numbers as a routine to develop concentration and memory.

Take a quick test how many of your classmates you remember from your high school and recollect their faces and associate the same with their names

Chapter 8

BECOME SUCCESSFUL WITH POWER GOALS

Goal Setting

How do you set goals and achieve them? The goals that you choose should synchronize with your inner urge, inborn talents and natural inclination to do something in preference to all the rest. You should set your goals yourself; no one should suggest this to you. You would be able to enjoy every moment of your wakeful state with the kind of activity that you simply enjoy doing.

The goals can be internal. Internal goals are intended to develop certain desirable habits and virtues and external goals are chosen to achieve something worthwhile and outstanding in life. Goals must be specific – dream to have wealth, good family, a lucrative job, enjoy scintillating health and in general a happy life. Vague dreams and ambitious will lead you nowhere. With proper planning goals must be achieved with diligent execution short-term and long-term goals must be formulated with specific targets. Achieve these targets one step at a time.

Have a clear cut vision as to the type of person you should emerge within a period of ten to fifteen years from now. Have a burning desire to do something great in life.

Action Plan to Set Specific Goals and Achieve Them

If you want to succeed in life, the first step you should take is to set specific goals in life.

Unless you have specific aims and goals in life you would tend to drift. Many youngsters do not have any specific aim in life. They simply dream to have fabulous wealth, good family, a lucrative job, enjoy scintillating health and in general a happy life. It is similar to that of a person simply asking for a ticket at the railway station without mentioning the destination. Further, no one can get anything worthwhile in life overnight. They should be meticulously sought after with proper planning and achieve them with diligent execution.

You should have a clear cut vision in your mind as to the type of person you should emerge within a period of ten or fifteen years from now. Cultivate the "habit" of visualizing for a big future. The size of your thinking determines the level of your achievement. The goals that you choose should synchronize with your inner urge, inborn talents and natural inclination to do something in preference to all the rest. This cannot be offered to you either by psychologists or counselors. There should be a burning desire to achieve something great in life. Otherwise life will not be pleasant and adventurous. You would be able to enjoy every moment of your wakeful state with the kind of activity that you simply enjoy doing. It should never be a burden or work for you.

The moment you have specific goals in life, you generate perennial energy to accomplish your goals. When you are totally committed to achieve something your energy

WILL

level will be remarkable. If the goal you want to achieve is after your heart you will never experience even an iota of tiredness or boredom. This is the secret of all geniuses in this world who are able to contribute something substantial and wonderful of the benefit of mankind.

Your guiding principle should be to achieve your goal one step at a time. A great achievement is nothing but a series of small accomplishments achieved over a long period. Constantly have a burning desire to do something great in life and you are sure to ACHIEVE whatever you want through proper goal setting.

Achievement is what you can do or contribute at your level, whereas prosperity is what you get from the society for your achievement. It may be in terms of money, name, fame, award, or reward. The former is internal, within your control and the latter is external. While choosing an aim in life our main attention should be focused on achievements rather than on Prosperity. If we want to achieve something positive in life we should always be productive and creative at every second of our wakeful state. We should constantly saturate our attention on acquiring knowledge and developing skills in the field in which we are deeply interested, based on our innate talents and abilities.

Different Types of Goals

Goals can be broadly divided into two categories, namely, Internal and External.

Internal goals are intended to develop certain desirable habits and virtues like honesty, sincerity, punctuality, purity, hard work, etc. You can set goals to develop such qualities and character and thereby improve your personality. This is one of the essential requisites for success in life.

External goals are chosen to achieve something great and outstanding in life. They deal with your contribution to the society. For example, writing a book, establishing an institution, serving the society as a good professional like doctors, engineers, teachers, lawyers, singers, actors, etc.

The goals can also be short-term and long-term. The short term goals are to be achieved within a short spell of time, say within a week or within a few months. Achieving your short term goals will enable you to attain your long term goals.

WILL

Long term goals determine your overall achievement in your life time. In the long run you will emerge as a person you would like to become.

Criteria for Choosing Your Goal

The goals that you choose should synchronize with your inner urge, innate talents and natural inclinations to do something. This cannot be offered to you either by psychologists or counselors. Everyone is a potential genius. Only a few realize their genius at an early age. They normally set goals based on their innate talents and achieve them.

Majority of the mankind are unaware of their innate potential. The best way for you to realize your own potential is to look at your past.

Understanding one's own potential and setting goals should go hand in hand. In the initial stage of setting goals you should devote at least 10 to 15 minutes in reflection of your past. Many of the events happened in your life may provide you a pattern of your talents and skills exhibited by you. You will be able to discover some of the activities that you love to do.

Goal Setting in Different Dimensions of Your Life

Goals can be formulated for different areas of your activities such as personal goals, professional goals, educational goals, financial goals, family goals, social goals, etc. **Professional** goals can also be formulated to reach a certain professional status; get promoted to a higher level; take up greater responsibility; pick up a project and try to complete within a stipulated time frame; acquire new skills in the professional field, etc.

Educational goals can be to pursue further studies, joining evening college; undertaking a course of studies in which you are interested.

Financial goals will indicate the amount to be earned within a specified time frame; get advanced to a higher salary level, chalk out an investment plan to suit your income level.

Family goals may be framed to improve the relationship within the family members, educational plans of the children, retirement plans, etc.

Social goals may be chalked out in respect of involving social services to the downtrodden people, help the handicapped, setting up some kind of an organization to render services to certain categories of people who are in need of help.

Personal goals are set up to improve one's own personality. This is similar to the internal goals. Some of the goals relating to personal area are: improving one's own health, developing sterling character and qualities, exercising daily, overcoming undesirable habits like smoking and drinking, etc.

Attributes of Goals and Objectives

The goals and objectives that you set should fulfill the following attributes: realistic, achievable, clear, specific, challenging, time-frame, consistent, quantifiable and written. If you set a goal to reach moon and settle down there, it is an unrealistic goal. As an individual it is an impossible task, on the other hand, it was possible for United States to send people to reach moon and get them back to earth.

While deciding the goals, your inner mind should inform you that the goal is REALISTIC and not simply a day dream. Every goal should be ACHIEVABLE from your point of you. You want to become the Prime Minister of

WILL

India. It may not be an unrealistic goal as people have become Prime Ministers before. As far as you are concerned, can you achieve this goal? This depends upon your situation and the profession that you embrace.

In order to become the Prime Minister, one of the essential requirements is to be in politics. If you are not in politics, your goal to become the Prime Minister becomes an unachievable goal.

Goals should be CLEAR and SPECIFIC. If you have a vague ambition that you want to become a learned person in life, it is neither clear nor specific. You should be very clear in which area you want to become learned. Again you must be very specific as to what you want to do to become learned. Your goal becomes specific when you decide to complete your M.A. in a specific subject.

The goals that you set should be CHALLENGING. Unless you have a challenging goals life will not be enchanting. There is great joy in doing something that ordinary people cannot do.

What is challenging for one person may not be so for someone else. Challenging goals are only relative. Goals should be achieved within a time frame.

WILL

Implementing the Goals

The successful implementation of the goals requires time. The way in which time should be spent for achievements of goals falls within your choice. After all life is a series of choices. The goals you have chosen are your own choices. Similarly, if you take a decision to implement the goals should also form part of your choice.

Writing goals down tends to make them more concrete and specific, helps you to have a clear vision about your future. The written goals are visual. This will motivate you to spend more time in achievement of these goals. You can gain a valuable new perspective by seeing your long cherished thoughts committed to paper. You can also comfortably examine your goals closely.

When the goals are in writing, they can be easily analyzed, redefined, changed and updated. Writing requires to be more specific. Your aims get narrowed down. There is great advantage in implementing the goals that are written down.

The successful implementation of the goals requires time. The way in which time should be spent for achievement of goals falls within your choice. After all life is a series of choices. The goals you have chosen are your own choices. Similarly, if you take a decision to implement the goals should also form part of your choice.

Have Smarter Goals

- Specific
- Measurable
- Achievable
- Realistic
- Timely
- Executable
- Reviewable

Goals can be sorted in five dimensions to impact results:

1. Faith
   (Faith is spiritual goal)
2. Family
   (Family is personal goal)
3. Finance
   (Finance is professional goal)
4. Fitness
   (Fitness is health goal)
5. Fun Goals
   (Fun is happiness goal)

Chapter 9

BECOME A SPORT AND DEAL WITH THE POWER OF HEALTH

Health impacts energy, Health is wealth. Health is everything.

If you have robust health, you will attract abundance by having focused action personally and professionally. Health is single most determining factor of stability, sustainability and success.

WILL

Requisites for Robust Health

Attitude: Have firm faith in the adaptive mechanism of the body. Do not y worry about health unnecessarily.

Diet: Eat when hungry. Eat plenty of seasonal fruits and vegetable; when ill, fast.

Sleep: Less sleep is better. Take short naps during the day, ranging from 7 to 70 minutes.

Practice Yoga regularly.

Energy: Have a clear goal. Live with happy frame of mind.

Nature's Cure: Avoid heavy medication Recourse to nature-cure methods, when ill.

Habits: Develop desirable habits and avoid detrimental ones.

Sex: Enjoy sex with a partner whom you love passionately.

Alpha Waves: Try to be always in Alpha Waves.

The best rule for robust health is moderation in everything you do and feel.

WILL

How should one develop a vibrant self- image?

Self-image is your own conception of the sort of person you are. You build a picture of yourself which you believe is true. All your actions and emotions are consistent with your self-image. Self-image can be changed for the better.

Never undervalue yourself.

You have something good to offer.

You are unique, neither superior nor inferior to anyone.

The aim of self-image psychology is to find out the best we have and to bring it out into the open.

You must listen to use your great creative mechanism as a success mechanism.

See yourself as a success - keep this image alive.

Your new picture to yourself will become a reality.

Accept your limitations and live each day with great spirit.

Stop holding grudges against others and against yourself.

WILL

Set goals that are reasonable but don't underrate your potential.

Think for yourself and ask for yourself what it is you want to achieve.

Life should be a process of continuing growth until death.

Believe in yourself.

The whole business of being successful is to rise above failure - to achieve success by overcoming failure and rising above it is a far greater victory, for in that very act you improve your self-image.

Action Plan to Generate Perennial Flow Of Energy

Choose a specific aim in life. There will be perennial flow of energy throughout your life. As long as your objectives are kept alive, the energy flow would be continuous. Realize the fact that energy is not sold in the form of pills or tablets or lotions. It flows from your thought patterns.

WILL

Start on a new project. Energy would flow endlessly. Tiredness is a disease. It does not come from a virus. It comes from boredom, lack of interest, a need for a goal, a target in life. As long as we love and appreciate life, we continue to enjoy the ever flowing energy. One of the ways to conserve energy is to keep silence and avoid unnecessary talk. It is not the physical frame of the body that produces more or less of energy, but the mental state of equipoise – a happy, joyous and meaningful direction produces more energy in a person. Mind never gets old. However, if it is not activated through constant work it may become inactive. Busy mind never ages.

When a person has an irresistible desire to accomplish a goal in life, he would be supplied with perennial flow of energy. Self-confidence generates energy. It comes from preparedness. Have a daily target of work to be done and you will have endless energy to accomplish the task on hand. Energy builders are happiness, laughter, love, affection, kindness, helping others, agreeability, hope and confidence. People who have abundant energy are less prone to suffer from diseases caused by stress.

A young person rushes to old age the moment he feels that he has nothing to do in this world. Secret of being energetic is in proper planning of each day. People with

WILL

concrete vision in life generate the energy to get things done. So to stimulate energy, day dream!

Three reasons to cause executives to lose energy are:

Fear to accept responsibility

Fear to delegate authority

Fear of sickness

Lack of energy does not go down the hereditary line.

Music restores energy. Fear of failure robs you of your energy. The more a person pursues his target in life the greater would be the energy his thought waves would produce. Mind is a great control box over the body. It can generate energy for you or drain it off, depending upon the nature of your thoughts. Successful living means perennial flow of energy in a person. People who must constantly make decisions of what to eat, wear each day burns up needless energy.

Some of the de-energizing mental blocks are: My mate is not faithful - My sex drive is failing - My friends are not true - My life is useless, etc.

WILL

It is experimentally proved that man does not expend any energy during mental work. Learn the art of keeping busy. Activity generates energy. Do the things you like.

Action Plan for Better Health

I will now give you some simple home remedies to deal with common everyday problems.

Headache: Take plenty of *grape juice to remove one-sided* headache.

Make a paste of salt and pepper and apply on the forehead to get relief from simple headache.

Equal quantities of cardamom, betel leaves and clove are ground into paste and applied on the forehead. Cut a betel leaf into two halves lengthwise, gently warm the leaves over the fire and apply over both the right and the left temple.

To get rid of *headache associated with cold and nasal* congestion, a paste of turmeric powder, a pinch of quick lime with milk or water is applied over the nose, temples and forehead.

Prepare a paste of betel leaves, pepper and boiled rice

(not cooked), the paste is heated in a small vessel, get it cooled and applied on the forehead (a tested method).

Heart Problems: To strengthen the heart: Prepare decoction out of white lotus petals, mix this decoction with milk and drink this in the morning and evening.

One teaspoon of tulsi juice and honey may be taken in the morning and evening.

Before going to bed drink cow's milk in which add the powder of gallant (*Harara*).

Honey and lemon juice be added in hot water, taken before going to bed.

A mixture of gooseberry juice (*Amla*) and cow's ghee is a good tonic for heart.

Liberal use of onion and garlic is said to be good for heart problems –

Burn a silk cloth and the ash is taken in honey.

Eat dates regularly.

Piles: *Hirupalathi* (an Ayurvedic medicine) may be taken in hot water.

WILL

Fry garlic in ghee, mix this in rice and eat.

White onions shredded and fried in ghee may be taken as such or mixed with rice.

eat one gram of powdered gallnut (*Harara*) daily along with a little old jaggery moistened with water if necessary.

Sexual Virility: Prepare powder out of cardamom and take at 3 grams in the morning and evening for a week only.

Take Tulsi seeds, soak them in water over night, pound them in the morning, mix in milk and take in empty stomach.

Eat plenty of well ripped plantain.

Drumstick leaves and flowers in any form.

Garlic and onion helps sexual virility.

Ginseng tea or capsule.

To prolong sexual activity: Take raw drumstick, open & insert tender areca nut, bind the drumstick with thread, cover with red clay, keep it for two months. Then take the areca nut & eat. Its antidote is lemon juice.

Smoking: To neutralize the bad effects of smoking- smokers, snuffers and tobacco eaters should frequently eat pineapple so that the bad effects of nicotine poison are neutralized.

You would be happy and content and burn up less energy. The best way to energetic life is to meditate.

Sleeplessness: Boil milk and add with it *khus khus* powder and drink this before going to bed.

Eat raw onion at supper time.

Bhakya kumbhaka meditation would help immensely for sleeplessness conditions.

Ulcer: Coconut and coconut milk.

Soup of cabbage, also take plenty of fruits and vegetables in all form.

BE SOCIAL AND OPEN UP TO THE WONDERS OF YOGA

A woman is a dignified person who occupies a special position in society. As a person she dons so many roles

WILL

like daughter, sister, and daughter in law, wife, mother, aunt, friend, mother-in-law and grandmother many a times she is on par with professionals like doctors, bureaucrats, scientists, spiritual human and counselors. She lives up to that reputation and and does all the best possible things for her family and loved ones.

She is the symbol of love, the roles she plays in the journey called life demands her energy and time. She is giving and forgiving. At times, the people who receive support and quickly forget about it. So here, I would like to inspire women in all age groups to embrace yoga and meditation. Meditation does wonders for you. It gives you an ideal balance and abundance.

Our prospective role play takes more of our time and energy and to be efficient in whatever we do, Yoga and meditation will be an effective way, if we can take care of our mental and physical personality, and we are doing ourselves a favor. Our aim must be to:

1. *Dress up* to the occasion and always be *cheerful*.
2. Be happy and *open-minded*.
3. Be *Knowledgeable* keep learning new things. *Network and* synergize with colleagues, business owners, entrepreneurs, etc.

4. Be *compassionate* and be equipped for eventualities.

One of the must have for WE GIRLS, I address women of every age group, and I stress that we should be in the mental horizon of18 years of age because our physical body does not grow beyond 18, expect the capacity to add mass. Similarly, we should consider ourselves as 18 years of age in our mental horizon. The plus years can be added as experience.

The message is loud and clear, every gentleman and family adores a woman who is happy, loving and considerate. Let's have focus in life - with the sole intention of BRINGING ABOUT A TRANSFORMATION IN THE SOCIETY by doing our bit for the society.

The best way to give back to society is spread love by being active.

We must understand the more we contribute to the society the better it gets. Take a sharp look at the mirror and say I have *the power to change* the way I look, dress and behave. Today is the first day for the rest of my life. From today I commit to Yoga and meditation for life. Because I understand that is the basic I can gift myself for the better me.

WILL

Dear Woman,

We must have a me time, we get 24 hours a day in that we need to have an hour as me time and do what makes us happy. *Make a conscious choice to be happy.*

I recommend you take an hour for yoga and meditation for a month and experience the difference, transformation becomes unstoppable.

Once you start liking it and get a hang of it you may give sessions as a return gift to the society for 30, 60 or 90 minutes to maximize your true potential.

I give you a small summary of yoga and meditation so that you are inspired to be at it for life and celebrate life.

Advantages of Meditation

The advantages are numerous, which are:

Slows down metabolic rate; heart rate slows down; blood flow increases; lactic acid effectively removed, when one is calm and serene lactic acid production is less. Presence of lactic acid is the symptom of blood pressure. Reduces blood pressure; improved dealing in psychosomatic diseases; improves intelligence, memory and emotional stability. Mental discipline; Better relaxation in sleep; inner peace and harmony; changes take place for better with regard to production of Alpha Waves, blood pressure and pulse rate.

Impact in curing incurable diseases, e.g. Dr. Carl Simonton cured many terminal cancer patients through CRVR meditation techniques: C for conviction, R for Relaxation through meditation, V for visualization, and R for Radiation treatment.

What are the Practices and Benefits of Pranayama?

1. Mukha Bhastika Pranayama - Ventilates and cleans, stimulates the cells and gives a general tone to the respiratory organs.
2. Ujjai Pranayama – Relieves coughing, aerates the lungs, removes phlegm, soothes the nerve and tones the entire system. Good for persons suffering from high blood pressure , intake of prana is higher.
3. Nadi Shodhana Pranayama – purifies nadis (subtle channels through which prana travels). Brings calmness and tranquility. Blood system is purified of toxins, activates right and left

hemispheres of the brain due to alternate breathing

4. Kapalabhati Pranayama – Cleanses the skull portion, activates the brain cells. Improves memory and intelligence. Purifies respiratory system and nasal passages, asthma is relieved, carbon dioxide is eliminated. Prevents the growth of grey hair.
5. Bhandhatreya Pranayama – Brings strength and vitality, preserves excess prana in the solar plexus. Healthy life all your life

What are Asanas?

They are yogic exercises. A person is required to keep the body in a particular position. There are 84,000 Asanas, of which only one Asana is sufficient to maintain excellent health. That is Sooryanamaskar.

What are the General Benefits of Asanas?

They cater to the development of both body and mind and impart control over the involuntary muscles of one's organism. Constant practice of Asanas will bring the following benefits: Flexibility to the body, digestion improves, mind becomes alert and agile, peace of mind

WILL

Concentration and self-control-brings about nervous equilibrium, develops sense of balance. Tones the spinal nerves; imparts a glow to the skin, clears the complexion. Elimination of waste from the body is improved and thus the likelihood of disease reduced. The sexual and generative organs are kept in good condition; retards obesity. Increases blood supply to the whole body and thereby strengthens the heart, lungs, liver, stomach, kidneys and bowels. Prevents and cures all diseases. A perennial flow of energy – it awakens kundalini. Ensuring complete relaxation and ease, it is the best antidote for the stresses of modern life.

What are the Techniques to Awaken Kundalini Shakti: Kundalini is a symbolic version of the vast potential energy and power embedded in every human being. When it is properly understood and directed to perform at its peak, the person will experience unimagined heights of perception and awareness. All geniuses in this world have tapped this potential energy for their stupendous accomplishments. The following techniques are used to awaken Kundalini (potential energy).

"All practices in the form of Japa, meditation, prayer, development of all virtues are at best calculated only to awaken this serpent power (kundalini) and make it pass through all the succeeding charkas – from Muladhara to Sahasrara"

Swami Sivananda

Practice Asana and Pranayama. Through constant practice of Yoga and Meditation the practitioner is expected to transcend his personality from the grossest manifestation of worldly desires, passions and instincts to that of the subtlest one of the intuition, inspiration, creativity and bliss which are the gateways to spiritual emancipation.

Kundalini can be awakened by:

Karma Yoga: passionate desire for creative activity.

Bhakthi Yoga: through developing love and affection for everybody, without discrimination.

Jnana Yoga: through understanding the mysterious phenomenon of nature and with total surrender to God and, also.

Raja Yoga: through mental discipline by following the path of eight steps of yogic practices. Only Raja yoga prescribes the techniques of Asana Pranayama, concentration and meditation to awaken kundalini. Sign

WILL

up for three months and you can master the art of yoga and meditation.

Personality is the total you it includes your senses, habits, thinking, attitude, skills and also feelings. All this must also be developed.

The following needs to be practiced in all aspects:

Integrity – this is what will constitute who you are, whether you are a working woman or a "Home Minister", be careful how you build your name in the family, within the extended family, friends, relatives, business connections, etc. Everywhere integrity is the key.

Punctuality – be on time, every time and preferably well beforehand (maybe 15 minutes).

Honesty – do what you have to do whether others are there are not, assume that you are collective to your conscience.

Spirituality – you must be highly spiritual and must embrace the path of God. Like me, you can chose to put your life in auto-pilot mode with Almighty. Have good faith in him and only focus on the good.

WILL

Reliability – you must be trustworthy. Trust must be inbuilt, be like a goddess, feel like a goddess and behave like one. Remember Goddess are ever giving. Givers Gain

Flexibility – practice to be like a river, and go with the flow without making any compromise. Be with the flow, go with the flow. Wash out everything which does not add value to you or your well being.

Credibility – you must be worth being called a gem and have worth. Be done and dusted with unproductive assignments, negative people and build your credibility right from the scratch.

You can create love with love only, not hatred; do small things with great love all the time.

We have only one life and remember we all are walking towards the grave all the time. I recommend we all should love, learn and leverage and to do this we must accept, adapt, adjust, appreciate and have a right attitude.

Life is short, but learning is long and continuous, be a student for life and be prepared to learn, unlearn and relearn life itself.

WILL

Life is a celebration, celebrate life, forgive quickly, love deeply, and come what may get up, dress up and show up. I wish you transformation and good luck on daily basis

Remember, the maximum we all may live is for 80 years, if we divide our life in multiples of 8; we realize the first 8 years were light years, we were unaware of surroundings and in the next 8 years we were establishing our identity by taking our score, assessing our intelligence quotient in high school examination; the next step would be to find a suitable life partner and settle down or use this time to establish professional stability.

By the time we are 32 years we have children and and by 40 we determine are we successful or not. Sometimes life may start at 40. Consider today the first day for the rest of your life.

Upto 40 your body takes care of you. And from here on it's your responsibility. Health is the most important factor now. Follow rituals and the next 8 years will be of practice will be rewarding. Being a woman, we need to work on relationships, sustainability, our life partner, and march towards peace - spreading love, cheer, joy and happiness wherever we go.

WILL

I recommend we need to do this in all stages of life. Network more; gain emotional stability; love life; become aware of your strengths, weaknesses, opportunities and threats; and work on building a better you. I am sure these simple tools will help build a dynamic you.

Have a brilliant life, and that starts from having a brilliant mindset.

All the best! Happy transformation!

O woman you are not only wonderful, you also own spectacular wisdom, believe in your powers, discover them and execute.

YOU WILL, WE WILL!

You Can Win, Never Give UP!

www.ingramcontent.com/pod-product-compliance
Lightning Source LLC
Chambersburg PA
CBHW071430180526
45170CB00001B/282